THE NEGRO FACES AMERICA

By

HERBERT J. SELIGMANN

Formerly Member of the Editorial Staffs
of *The New York Evening Post*
and *The New Republic*

ISBN: 978-1-63923-820-0

Printed: March 2023

Published and Distributed By:
Lushena Books
607 Country Club Drive, Unit E
Bensenville, IL 60106
www.lushenabks.com

ISBN: 978-1-63923-820-0

CONTENTS

FOREWORD

I SHOULD apologize for so impressionistic a study as this of American color problems, if apologies were in order. But social science, such as it is, has evaded the subject. Much of what has been offered to lay readers calls to mind the acrid comment of Mr. Van Wyck Brooks that "to be a prophet in America it is not enough to be totally uninformed; one must also have a bland smile." I should like to banish the bland smile from discussion of American color problems and to challenge the shabby indifference with which the wrongs of colored people in the United States are greeted.

With this humane intent my expositions and my interpretations are perhaps complicated. If the result be a clearer field than has existed heretofore for research and social invention, I shall consider the polemic elements in a work, which should have been undertaken by a trained sociologist, to have been not wholly unjustified. In extenuation for having written I have no plea except that of my observations, which must be judged accurate or inaccurate on their merits. For much of the material which made those observations possible I am indebted to the officers and to members of the staff of the National Association for the Advancement of Colored People.

H. J. S.

May 22, 1920.

INTRODUCTION

The uniqueness and pathos of the Negro problem in the United States rest in the fact that so few Americans recognize it as a problem. The average attitude is that a pretty good job is being made of a very trying situation; as to the occasional suggestion of possible tragic developments in the future, unless the whole matter is definitely taken in hand, a flippant and naïve remark as to the valor of American manhood is usually deemed sufficient. Among the more serious agencies at work, aiming at a more enlightened attitude toward the race problem, may be mentioned the intensely race-conscious activity of DuBois and the broader and less emotionalized activity, on a national basis, of Spingarn. To these must now be added the name of Mr. Herbert J. Seligmann, the young author of this volume.

In close touch with the scientific and social facts, the author reviews the conclusions of anthropologists with reference to alleged racial differences in capacity, analyzes the social and psychological factors at work in different parts of the country where the race question is acute, lays bare the sinister influence of selfish and callous individuals on whom must in large measure rest the responsibility for the more tragic aspects of the Negro situation, and by his sympathetic and obviously open-minded attitude toward the future almost succeeds in creating a definitely optimistic mood.

It is to be hoped that this will not be the last of the author's contributions, and that he will before long have the opportunity to deal with ever-increasing technical skill, with the several special aspects of the Negro problem which have long been awaiting an enthusiastic, able, and courageous protagonist.

A. A. GOLDENWEISER.

The New School for Social Research,
NEW YORK.

THE NEGRO FACES AMERICA

THE NEGRO FACES AMERICA

I

THE BLIND SPOT

INTO the nerve fiber of the United States are woven strands which bind Negro and white Americans. The Civil War lacerated the nation's nervous system. Slight occasion only is needed in order to recall suffering and hatred to memories still fiercely active. The condition of public feeling with regard to race is one of disease. The past lives on unconquered and poisons the present. Slavery is legally abolished, but neither white men nor Negro men are free of a constant preoccupation with color. It is still possible to divide public opinion in the United States with regard to race problems on the artificial basis of geography, and this division is reinforced by tradition. A vast discussion goes on, punctuated by race riots and lynchings, thunderous with invective, in which the conversational tone of the scientist is almost inaudible. Many of the disputants' feelings, passionately intense, colored with every sort of gossip, rumor, and half-truth, never find their way to frank expression in words. The emotions that have been at one time or another fanned into flame as between white man and Negro; conflicts over field, shop, and factory; pride of race and assertions of human prerogatives; the rights of man and the defense of womanhood; education, political contest, the home, public travel, have all become involved. Last of all, the emergence of the United States from her "splendid isolation" through war into the desolation of a crumbling world has been accompanied by new and ominous twinges in the nerves of race relations.

It would be difficult, if not impossible, to point to a single political or social problem of importance in the United States which does not debouch upon race and what by common consent is known as "the" race problem. School, home, factory, mine, farm, the polling-booth, the railway, are all made its vehicles. Every manifestation of the social will hesitates at the inevitable race considerations.

This welter has been lumped into a "problem" whose symbol is black. Those who wear the burnished livery of the sun have been dehumanized and made into problems also—from twelve million to fifteen million problems, children in the cradle, school boys and girls, men and women. Negro Americans, on the other hand, fiercely resent being looked upon as a problem. They feel themselves to be a challenge that may well become retribution. The challenge of the race problem confronts all Americans, white and black, North and South. Few Southerners but have learned the history of New England merchant captains' adventures in rum and slaves on the west coast of Africa or have forgotten the memorable carrying trade. The Negro is constantly reminded that what he does or fails to do is visited upon his race, and that he is his colored brother's keeper. The white man of the North, who might be inclined to lull himself into forgetfulness, wakes at the sound of shooting down his streets. He has heard echoes of race and the race problem in the speeches of United States Senators discussing the League of Nations. Any one even slightly informed of American institutions, traditions, politics, art, society, has known that all the nation has been in the same boat with regard to the race problem. The United States has at various times been known abroad as the nation of jazz. It is not only the antagonisms of race that make the land conscious of itself; its arts and its amusements have begun to feed this consciousness. In no activity is art so near to amusement and amusement so near art as in the peculiar rhythms of American Negro song. Unfortunately, before it was realized that Americans cannot afford to be cosmopolitan when they speak of commerce, and parochial when they think and speak of race, race relations had to be made into melodrama. In a world composed for the most part of colored races, fully embarked on new adventures toward autonomy, Americans had to be reminded not only by a great northward migration of colored people during the war, but by race riots, chiefly in 1919, that new movements and aspirations were stirring on their own continent. It was blood-letting in the streets of American cities that accomplished anxious heart-searchings that were long overdue.

A first step in an attempt upon the hates, distrusts, and preconceptions clustered about race is to separate and examine them. There is, in fact, no race problem in the United

States. There are a thousand problems with which race is more or less connected, frequently deliberately connected for an ulterior motive, in the absence of organic connection between race distinctions and the subject at issue. To take these thousand problems of education, politics, industry, and lump them is to give over to emotion what should be the province of study and social invention. The process is best illustrated by two questions: "Do you want your daughter to marry a nigger?" is a Southern summation of and for white men. That is a reduction of the race problem to what many conceive to be its lowest and most fundamental terms. "Shall I be set apart like a leper, insulted, denied justice, and lynched because I am accused of wanting to marry the white man's daughter?" retorts the Negro. "And shall the white man have children by my daughter and be prohibited by law from marrying her?" To leave race relations at this point is to create an impasse. There is no answer to either of the questions. If every time the Negro demands better housing and schooling for his children, justice in the courts, equal opportunity for employment, he is to be denied them on the ground that it means race amalgamation, there is nothing for it but to leave the issue to arms and to maintain a white army sufficient to keep the subject race in subjection. Fortunately there is much evidence that race problems are not merely biological, that they are susceptible to social invention and intelligent manipulation. Such evidence was presented as perhaps never before in the race riots that occurred in the United States during and immediately after the end of the World War.

If white Americans are minded to accept the evidence so crudely offered, they may be in a position to absorb consciously, as they have not done, the cultural contributions of their colored neighbors. Colored Americans may then be liberated from the pressure which no one realizes better than their own leaders is cramping their efforts, making them provincial and yet critically aloof, bitterly conscious of themselves as a hostile group in an ill-ordered community. Granted that there are distrusts and hostilities that come of superficial differences between men, like color, or like follicular structure of the hair differentiating kinky from straight, it is a savage thing for white men who call themselves civilized to let such primitive impulses determine their conduct. Yet the history of race relations in the United States, a history only as yet included in larger and more diffuse studies, or suggested in biographies, essays, and memoirs, will show the dominance of these primitive impulses in an attack upon the nation's deepest-rooted and most pressing difficulties.

To those who insist that racial antipathies must be allowed to determine race relations there are two replies: First, that to do so brings, as it has brought, violence. Second, that there is overwhelming evidence to show that race antipathy is not even skin deep. The decrease in illicit sex relations between white and colored people of the South, where intermarriage is illegal, is due not to instinctive aversion, but to the pressure of public opinion. When it used to be regarded as an entertaining foible for white men of prominence to maintain colored families without benefit of clergy, the practice was fairly common. Now that exposure of such relationships would ruin any aspirant's political and social career, white men are more wary and illicit relationships of the sort are said to be decreasing in number. A dangerous error of persons who insist on the validity of "racial antipathy" is to assume that the exceptional conditions which prevail in the United States are typical. But nowhere else have economic considerations and race relations been joined as issues in armed conflict as in the Civil War. Of Latin America, Professor Shepherd tells us that "properly speaking there is no race question . . . because from the colonial period onward the ethnical elements have tended to become merged into a new division of mankind."[1] In the circumstances it is incumbent on the upholders of racial antipathy's function in a democracy to show that it is operative and effective.

Much of the bitterness that has befogged discussion of race problems has proceeded from observations honestly made in past years, but since discredited by anthropologists. Many passionate Unionists, during the Civil War even, were convinced of an essential "racial inferiority" of the Negro, and allowed their beliefs, on which investigation has thrown new light, to erect obstacles to Negro participation in the state and in society. No less a contributor to our knowledge than Louis Agassiz wrote in 1863 that

[1] William R. Shepherd, *Latin America*, p. 123. New York: Henry Holt & Co.

on Egyptian monuments "the Negroes are so represented as to show that in natural propensities and mental abilities they were pretty much what we find them at the present day—indolent, playful, sensual, imitative, subservient, good-natured, versatile, unsteady in their purpose, devoted, and affectionate. . . . While Egypt and Carthage grew into powerful empires and attained a high degree of civilization; while in Babylon, Syria, and Greece were developed the highest culture of antiquity, the Negro race groped in barbarism and never originated a regular organization among themselves." The conclusions of Agassiz left him unprepared "to state what political privileges they are fit to enjoy now; though I have no hesitation in saying that they should be equal to other men before the law." [1]

But since 1863 the sciences of men have become distrustful of "natural propensities"; and even of races which have been most carefully studied anthropologists hesitate to say what are their racial characteristics. Furthermore, modern anthropology does not credit white men with having changed racially,

[1] James Ford Rhodes, *History of the United States*, Vol. VI, Chap. XXXI, letter from Agassiz to Dr. Samuel G. Howe. 1863. Pp. 37, 38.

in so far as their natural propensities are concerned, since the Egyptian artificers made the monuments to which Agassiz refers. It would be as fair to deduce the disposition of present-day white men from monuments contemporaneous with those erected by the Pharaohs as to attach significance to the characters of ancient sculptured Negro faces. Comment of which that of Agassiz is typical still passes current, however, and is given the force of dogma by those predisposed to it.

Many of the dogmas about the Negro which find astonishingly wide acceptance are of such general and inclusive nature that they can be immediately disposed of. For example, the one which has it that the Negro is by nature indolent and lacking in persistence, because he comes of a savage race and savages have those characteristics, is not borne out by observation. Savages of many tribes in various parts of the world display extraordinary pertinacity. With inferior implements they laboriously achieve results which the white man would hesitate to attempt because of the sustained and arduous labor involved. To cut down a tree with stone hatchets and then to make a canoe from the trunk by burning out the core is no task for the indolent or the man of unsteady purpose. All of the beliefs held about the Negro by white men, more or less misinformed, constitute one of the main problems of race in the United States. It is a problem intensified rather than lessened by such means of communication as the press. Whether or not the Negro is what his bitterest enemy says of him hardly matters. If any body of public opinion can be organized upon misstatements as a foundation, all public discussion will be colored by the most obvious fabrications and absurdities.

There is the utmost hesitance, for example, to trace to its lair the gossip from Civil War days which still lives on. The nation is expected, when enforcement of the Fifteenth Amendment to the United States Constitution is suggested, to thrill with horror at the mere thought of "Negro domination" in the South. If Negroes were conceived to be human beings like many another human being, educable and educated, adapted to the processes of American government and appreciative that liberty for oneself implies liberty for others, Negro domination would have no immense terrors. But paint the Negro's portrait as of a sullen black brute, criminal when he has opportunity to be, intent upon debasing the limpid intellectuality of the superior race by admixing his own base blood, desirous chiefly of dining with the white man and of marrying his daughter, incapable of intellectual development after he has reached the age of fourteen years, then you have laid the basis for assertions like that of Senator John Sharpe Williams, that race transcends the Constitution; and for sympathetic response to the statement that, come what will, no Negro will ever vote in a state like South Carolina, where in 1910 there were 835,843 Negroes and 679,161 white men. Of misinformation and terror it is difficult to say which has played the greater part in preventing a decent adjustment of the Negro's claims to the ballot and to other prerogatives of citizenship.

It is possible to take any group of a race, as is frequently done in the case of Negroes, and point to its members as uneducated, vagrant, unfit for civic responsibilities. But to erect the ignorance of men, to whom their state has denied education, into a threat of domination by the ignorant and the brutal is as fantastic as to say that ignorance is proof of the uselessness of education. Such absurdities would hardly be the province of serious discussion of race relations if they did not frequently even yet form the body of discussion in many parts of the United States. Much water has run under many bridges since President Andrew Johnson and a Congress he antagonized bungled the matter of readjusting the seceded Southern states to the Union.

But the South to-day still feeds upon the stories of carpet-bagger dominion, the "black and tan" Constitutional Convention of Mississippi with its extravagance, and the financial orgies of Louisiana and South Carolina legislatures. Historians of the first rank, even, have not escaped the tendency to touch lightly the pride and the humiliation of men who found their former slaves not only no longer their possessions—an economic loss—but were expected to tolerate disfranchisement while those abhorred men voted. The present generation is in danger of hardening reticence into doctrine, of making monuments of past sorrows and humiliations which bar the way to effective discussion and progress. If, as is asserted, carpet-bag rule and the participation of uneducated Negroes in state government resulted in tragic waste and terrible conditions of social disorganization, it must still be borne in mind that men blame what they oppose for all their misfortunes rather than trace those misfortunes dispassionately to their source. With all the suffering and the losses imposed upon the South—as upon any region in which war is waged—the offer of Congress to the Southern states, "compared with the settlement of any other notable civil war by a complete victor," as James Ford Rhodes points out, was "magnanimous in a high degree. It involved no executions, no confiscation of property, no imprisonments. . . . It vouchsafed to the Southern states the management of their own local affairs subject to the recognition of the civil rights of the Negroes, to the Freedmen's Bureau limited in time, and to a temporary military occupation." History is irrelevant except as it continues to live on in the present. And Rhodes's characterization of the attitude of the former slaveholders toward the Negro is significant in this discussion. Pointing out that the slaveholder did not hate the Negro, he continues, "They did not believe that he could rise in the scale of civilization, nor did they wish him to rise, and they were indignant at the mention of a possible political or social equality." This attitude was made effective, according to the report which Carl Schurz sent the President. Of the people of the South, he said, that "while accepting the 'abolition of slavery,' they think that some species of serfdom, peonage, or other form of compulsory labor is not slavery and may be introduced without a violation of their pledge. Although formally admitting Negro testimony, they think that Negro testimony will be taken practically for what they themselves consider it 'worth.'"[1] The so-called "Black Codes" would have perpetuated what the moral judgment of the nation and the decision of arms had condemned. By act of the Mississippi legislature of 1865 a poll tax of one dollar was imposed upon Negroes between the ages of eighteen and sixty. "Failure to pay the tax," says Garner, "was to be deemed *prima facie* evidence of vagrancy, and it was made the duty of the sheriff to arrest the offender and hire him out for the amount of the tax plus the costs. . . . Civil officers were required to arrest freedmen who should run away from their contracts and carry them

[1] James Ford Rhodes, *History of the United States,* Vol. V, Chap. XXX, p. 553.

back to the place of employment."[1] The Black Codes, says Mr. Paul Leland Haworth, "were in part an honest effort to meet a difficult situation, but the old slavery attitude toward the Negro peered through most of them and gave proof that their framers did not yet realize that the old order had passed away."[2] That old orders do not speedily pass away has been almost too often demonstrated, especially when the old order is so inwoven in current thought and utterance that its influence is to most persons imperceptible. To an extent that few Americans realize the old order persists. It is justified on the ground of a variety of necessities, and draws into its entanglements human and political relations of every sort. It can stand against law and legislation better than against pitiless statement and publication of fact.

If the Black Codes throw light on the opposition to the Negro's economic advancement which persists to this day, present talk of Negro domination is illumined by the report of the joint committee of Congress

[1] James Wilford Garner, *Reconstruction in Mississippi*, 1901. New York: Macmillan Company. Pp. 114, 115.

[2] Paul Leland Haworth, *Reconstruction and Union, 1865-1912*, New York: Henry Holt & Co. P. 16.

into the activities of the Ku-Klux Klan. There is a wide divergence of opinion as to the justification for the outrages which were visited upon Unionists and Negro Republicans in the South. Justification is sought in the dangers from criminal vagrants, and the Ku-Klux bands who spread terror are compared with the *posse comitatus* of the West which rid the surrounding country of horse-thieves and gamblers. But the divergence of opinion extends even to Southerners. Without imputing exclusively political motives to the white brotherhood, it is still possible to question the necessity for what was done, to inquire if fear rather than fact was not its motive impulse. Gen. J. B. Gordon, who commanded the left wing of Lee's army at the surrender, was asked by the joint committee:

"Have the Negroes, as a general thing, behaved well since the war?"

His reply was, "They have behaved so well that the remark is not uncommon in Georgia that no race on earth, relieved from servitude under such circumstances as they were, would have behaved so well." [1]

[1] Report of the Joint Select Committee to Inquire into the Condition of Affairs in the late Insurrectionary States, 1872, Vol. I, p. 53. Washington: Government Printing Office.

The faith which Negro slaves kept with their masters absent in the war, caring for white families, guarding white women and children, is proverbial. Under the circumstances, the actions of the white South during Reconstruction are referable rather to emotion than to situations requiring drastic response.

"The excuse that the whites were goaded into such outrages by the evils of Negro domination," says Doctor Haworth of the Ku-Klux, "is true only in part, for the Klans displayed notable activity in opposing the new state constitutions and in the election of state officers before the blacks were yet in power."[1]

"The five and a half million whites," says Rhodes, "who were legislating for three and a half million blacks were under the influence of 'the black terror' which was not known and therefore not appreciated at the North. Many of the laws were neither right nor far-sighted, but they were natural." And then, as if to clinch the efficacy of the "terror" motive, he adds, "The enactments the least liberal as to civil rights and the most rigorous as to punishment of misdemeanors and crimes were those of South Carolina, Mississippi, and

[1] *Op. cit.,* pp. 44, 45.

Louisiana, in which states the proportion of Negroes to white men was the largest."[1] Situations change, but the style of argumentation on the race question seems forever to continue unchanged. In fifty-four years Negroes in the United States demonstrated that not only could they acquire the fundamentals of education necessary to participatiou in the processes of democratic government, but they have made progress that would be considered extraordinary when measured by any standards. Against the initial opposition and disbelief expressed in the Black Codes and subsequent disfranchisement in the Southern states; against the repression most violently imposed by the Ku-Klux and still a part of the code of many white Americans, they have with relentless determination built business enterprise, gone to the land and made it yield to them, fought their way by sheer work and talent into the closed ranks of the professions, furnished to the United States government district attorneys, consular and diplomatic officers, and against most determined opposition, military leaders and soldiers. In the commerce between cultured representatives of the Negro and white

[1] *Op. cit.*, Vol. V, Chap. XXX, p. 558.

races, where the Negro is freed from the attitude of defense and awkward apprehension, and the white man has progressed beyond the savage canon which says that strangers are enemies, a reciprocity becomes possible that has a slight zest of adventure and challenges perception. From the point of view of such friendships, which the Southern code would bar, distinctions of color are as extraneous as those of nationality. It is at once tragic and laughable that the meanest white man whose universe is bounded by his local newspaper and his own hates should take precedence over the colored student and artist; it is one of those ironies of which the world is prodigal that by a rigid dogma enforced with all the conviction of inquisition, bounds should be set to the work of the scientist, that people should be misinformed, hates perpetuated and introduced in new fields, creative spirits checked and frustrated. As the emphasis of the modern state shifts and inclines from political achievement to the task of freeing men from the imposition of the deadening task and the drudgery of overwork, there come to mind words spoken by Governor Humphreys of Mississippi in his inaugural of 1865:

"The Negro, he said, was free, whether the people liked it or not, but freedom did not make him a citizen or entitle him to political or social equality with white men." [1]

In those places where the Negro has achieved political equality with white men, that freedom still does not give him industrial equality. The Negro student of law, the university graduate, too often is free to vote in the same booth with the white man, but must seek employment as a Pullman porter. Of the denial of opportunity in the North which still prevails there is a survey in Miss Mary White Ovington's *Half a Man*.

Complications of political problems by passions rooted in race and sex are carried over into industry and for a time will make social organizations more difficult. If the prejudice against the Negro's voting and holding office is a matter of balance of power, the excuse being his alleged unfitness, the prejudice against him in industry will have to be met by extraordinary proof.

Unfortunately, the problem of the Negro's participation in political and civil life has seldom received precise formulation. It is admitted, though not universally, that he

[1] Garner. *Op. cit.*, p. 111.

should be the equal of the white man before the law. The inequality here is in part a corollary of the development of law and legal procedure as instruments of class. In part it is due to a habit of mind so inured to prejudice that injustice and discrimination become routine. The demands of the political state differ from the demand of blind justice whose unseeing gaze supposedly rests neither on dark skin nor meager purse. But the political state and democracy especially are entitled to no further questions than: Can you read and write? Are you capable of understanding the issues upon which, as an elector, you will be required to pass? With these questions the peculiar biological disposition of the Negro has nothing to do. Granted that he might in his own environment, played upon by streams of culture—the arts, literature, political thought—evolve a civilization different from the one in which he is placed. The question remains: Can and does the colored citizen of the United States conform to the minimum requirements of political democracy? If he can and does meet the test, which in effect asks him if he is a human being, by what justification is he deprived of his prerogative? To state the question is to answer it. Politics has no concern, under the theory which is supposed to dominate American procedure, with questions properly referable to anthropologists. Those questions, be it said, involve measurements and observations more delicate than would be conceded by the persons who invoke the questions. In the play of political life, which has consisted in endeavoring to make recalcitrant fact fit the mold of men's desire, the colored United States citizen has been the victim of extraneous issues, created and constantly invoked by those who in effect want to divorce the practice of American government from the affirmations upon which, presumptively, it rests.

Such discussion seems academic when it is opposed to the brute realities with which American public opinion is faced. Colored citizens of the United States are still publicly burned alive at the stake. Much editorial discussion states rather than implies that colored people are less than beasts of the field. Many a Mississippian will affirm, as the Jackson, Mississippi, *Daily News* did on June 20, 1919, "that the door of hope is forever closed to the Negro, in so far as partieipation in politics is concerned, and there is no appeal from that decree."

That remark was accompanied by a thinly veiled threat against a propaganda conducted by the "Lincoln League of America": "If this propaganda is to embrace the desire to vote, then it had better be located north of the Ohio River. It will not be safe in Memphis and its issuance of propaganda will be short-lived."

Propaganda embracing "the desire to vote" unsafe south of the Ohio River? The question is one which, if pursued, would throw much light on tolerance south of the Ohio River, and the effect of that peculiar sort of tolerance on the right to hold opinions and express them elsewhere in the United States. It will be observed that the discrimination is categorical—color divides the country. It is an unfortunate division to perpetuate in political and social life.

All human values are put in the scales that are tipped against the Negro. It is almost a commonplace of civilized dogma that the brutal man hurts himself more deeply than he does the object of his brutality. Yet this observation, typical of civilization, seems to have little practical effect on the conduct of many white Americans toward the Negro. Lynching, the public murder, often with unspeakable mutilations and torture, of colored men will be spoken of as though it occurred only in rural communities where social organization approximates that of frontiers throughout the world. But from this point of view a large portion of the United States still consists of frontier; its civilization is in the making. The country enjoyed the spectacle in July, 1919, of a Governor of Mississippi hesitating to prevent what was announced in glaring newspaper head-lines would be a burning at stake, on the ground that an overwhelming public sentiment in his state made him powerless. It matters little that the Negro was accused of "the one crime," rape. Even if, as one colored newspaper affirmed was the case, the victim had been guilty of attracting the regard of, and not of assaulting, a white woman, the penalty would still have been death. For with the rope, the torch, the pistol, that Negro is answered who so much as gives occasion for believing he has said an intimate word to a white woman. The attitude which prompts a spirited defense of such barbarity will have to be removed from the United States before this country can pretend to civilization. One effective means of removing it is to show it as a corollary of class exploitation of the Negro.

Garner[1] tells of the emigration which was urged by Confederate leaders, among them Gen. Sterling Price, who wrote from Mexico in December, 1865, "I pray to God that my fears for the future of the South may never be realized, but when the right is given to the Negro to bring suit, testify before the courts, and vote in elections, you all had better be in Mexico."

The objection is to the Negro's being accorded "political and civil rights."

"As soon as it became evident," says Garner, "that free Negro labor could be made profitable, and that the admission of the Negro to the witness-stand and the jury-box would not be accompanied by the terrible results predicted, the emigration movement died out entirely."

If there was reason for saying that the emigration movement was a "delusion gotten up for the benefit of speculators," fortified by a fear that free Negro labor could not be made "profitable," there is every reason now for believing that race antagonisms are fomented by those who exploit the Negro.

[1] *Op. cit.*, p. 134.

"The refusal of the legislature," says Garner, "to accord the Negro civil and political rights was, of course, due to prejudices and traditions which constituted a part of the very fabric of Southern society, and the sudden banishment of which was not an easy task."

Any society which profits from the labor of its members, denies them social privileges like education, proper sanitation, and decent housing, and denies civil prerogatives such as legal redress, may be said to be founded upon exploitation of those individuals. The reports of the Commissioner of Education and the mortality rates for Negroes are a commentary on the attention given the race as a group in the Southern states. To allow any man to work and produce and not to accord him the benefits and the protection of the society which he makes possible is a crude form of exploitation which, as regards the Negro, is still the rule rather than the exception.

W. D. Weatherford[1] has made quite clear the realization of a few progressive Southern white men that "if the Negro race is dying

[1] W. D. Weatherford, *Present Forces in Negro Progress*, 1912, pp. 73-74. New York: Association Press.

rapidly, the white man is responsible. I mean," he explains, emphatically, "in the country we give him so little training in the laws of hygiene that he does not know the art of self-preservation. I mean that we allow city landlords to build abominable huts in which the Negro has to live. We allow the streets in the section where he lives—even though within the city limits—to go without drainage, sewerage, paving, or even garbage service. We allow practices which no self-respecting community ought to allow, and all these things result in indifference, immorality, physical inability, and death for the Negro—and we are his murderers. . . . The truth is that in our day the criminal most to be feared is not the red-handed murderer or the pad-footed robber, but the men who, clothed in all their high respectability, sit in their fine offices and smile, while poor devils all around them are dying for want of protection from the greed of the money shark, the lust of the landlord, and the chicanery of the cheap politician."

The exploitation of the Negro in the United States is a procedure in which Northern and Southern white men have been jointly concerned. Every time a colored man is lynched or burned at stake, the entire nation participates through the press. Its indifference is in reality active tolerance. "Only a Negro," when it is applied to lynching, deadens spontaneous protest when the landlord terrorizes the Negro farm tenant or drives Negro labor, or when the white labor-unionist discriminates against the colored workman. "Only a Negro" becomes the excuse, the justification for every sort of injustice and oppression. Undertaken by individuals and groups of the community for their own gains, the exploitation is justified socially, tolerated by the community and the state, erected finally into a dogma which, when it is not upheld and defended, becomes a commonplace. Where there is not actual slavery in the form of terrorism, social discrimination, and absence of the flimsiest pretense at justice, it is potential in the indifference which prevails with regard to those practices. Freedom consists not in a law abolishing slavery. It consists in passionate and determined affirmation of the value of human lives as against the disposition to exploit human beings. It is as absurd to justify wretched housing for the Negro by saying that better housing means race amalgamation as it is to repeat the rapidly, the white man is responsible. I mean," he explains, emphatically, "in the country we give him so little training in the laws of hygiene that he does not know the art of self-preservation. I mean that we allow city landlords to build abominable huts in which the Negro has to live. We allow the streets in the section where he lives—even though within the city limits—to go without drainage, sewerage, paving, or even garbage service. We allow practices which no self-respecting community ought to allow, and all these things result in indifference, immorality, physical inability, and death for the Negro—and we are his murderers. . . . The truth is that in our day the criminal most to be feared is not the red-handed murderer or the pad-footed robber, but the men who, clothed in all their high respectability, sit in their fine offices and smile, while poor devils all around them are dying for want of protection from the greed of the money shark, the lust of the landlord, and the chicanery of the cheap politician."

The exploitation of the Negro in the United States is a procedure in which Northern and Southern white men have been jointly concerned. Every time a colored man is lynched or burned at stake, the entire nation participates through the press. Its indifference is in reality active tolerance. "Only a Negro," when it is applied to lynching, deadens spontaneous protest when the landlord terrorizes the Negro farm tenant or drives Negro labor, or when the white labor-unionist discriminates against the colored workman. "Only a Negro" becomes the excuse, the justification for every sort of injustice and oppression. Undertaken by individuals and groups of the community for their own gains, the exploitation is justified socially, tolerated by the community and the state, erected finally into a dogma which, when it is not upheld and defended, becomes a commonplace. Where there is not actual slavery in the form of terrorism, social discrimination, and absence of the flimsiest pretense at justice, it is potential in the indifference which prevails with regard to those practices. Freedom consists not in a law abolishing slavery. It consists in passionate and determined affirmation of the value of human lives as against the disposition to exploit human beings. It is as absurd to justify wretched housing for the Negro by saying that better housing means race amalgamation as it is to repeat the unverified and unverifiable gossip about "race inferiority" which was used to oppose the abolition of slavery in Civil War days. Any group which desires material advantage from the exploitation of another group always takes pains to characterize its victims as inferior. There have been times when Englishmen were as assured of the inferiority of the Irish, as many a white man now is about the "nigger." The Turk is doubtless convinced of the inferiority of the Armenian; the Magyar and the Czech, the Rumanian and the Magyar, the Polish noble and the Jew, all furnish examples of oppression justified by spurious "inferiorities." Under cover of these appeals to contempt and passion the human relations which make civilization possible are ruthlessly violated.

The United States has been paying the price for its misinformation about race relations and its indifference to the administration of those relations. It is not race riot so much as the spirit which is given rein and perpetuated in mob violence that is destructive of civilization. For every riot which has occurred in consequence of the fomenting of race hatred half a dozen have smoldered, ready to burst into conflagrations that would have consumed hundreds of lives. Many American cities have had all the elements provocative of race riot except the accident that brings about armed conflict. North and South may be divided by a difference in the intensity of feeling on race matters of their white and colored citizens, not by the incidence of riot.

It is asserted on the one hand that what creates race problems in the South is the Negro's absolute inferiority; on the other that race problems arise not by reason of the Negro's inherent character, but only where he is numerous. In fact, economic conditions play their part, and the consequence of economic conflict is to attach to racial distinction what does not properly belong to it. Thus, Phillips quotes John Adams as having written in 1795:

"Argument might have [had] some weight in the abolition of slavery in Massachusetts, but the real cause was the multiplication of laboring white people, who would no longer suffer the rich to employ these sable rivals so much to their injury. . . . If the gentlemen had been permitted by law to hold slaves, the common white people would have put the Negroes to death, and their masters, too, perhaps."[1]

The issue in Massachusetts, if we are to accept John Adams's statement, was not the rights of man or any ethical consideration, nor was it the inferiority or superiority of the black workman, his physical or other characteristics. It was, just as it was during the steel strike late in 1919, a question of the use by employers of one group of working-people to undercut the wages of another group. Disturbances such as occurred at the steel-plants were called race riots because the participants happened to differ in color. This, as will be developed in subsequent chapters, has often been the case. The expression of industrial, social, political conflict in "race riot" is only a crude demonstration of the fact that race hatred is a convenient and much-abused term used to describe desires far less unconscious and less defensible than race hatred is supposed to be.

What the course will be of race relations in the United States it would be hazardous to venture to predict. It can be said only that the information upon which most per-

[1] Ulrich Bonnell Phillips, *American Negro Slavery*, 1918. New York: D. Appleton & Co., p. 119.

sons form their judgments is inaccurate; that the forces which make for improved race relations have for the most part derived their support from a small number of individuals; and that almost every national social power, from the press to the United States army, including such agents of the state as the Department of Justice, the House of Representatives, and the Senate, contrives increasingly to becloud the issues underlying race conflict and to embitter feeling. On the other hand, the Negro's new importance to Northern industry, even as a weapon against white labor-unionism, will force white unionists, once they realize the folly of perpetuating the Negro workers' enmity, to accept him as one of themselves. In that event race relations will more obviously go into the phase of class conflict, in which economic position rather than race will determine men's attitudes. Meanwhile the point at which to arrest wasteful, violence-breeding conceptions is in childhood. To children prejudices are foreign and alien until they absorb them from parent or teacher. If ostracism were as swift and as certain for the white man who says what is demonstrably false about the Negro as for the man who upholds the Negro's claims to citizenship, the vexing and vexed "race problem" would soon cease to complicate every plan and activity of United States citizens.

II

WHY RACE RIOTS?

A PERSPECTIVE of recent American history reveals armed conflicts between white men and black, like beacon fires, serving as illuminants and as warnings. The summer and early fall of 1919 especially were distinguished by outbreaks which seemed to many a portent of race war to come. In June bloody conflict raged in Longview, Texas, bursts of fire spat from houses in which colored men defended themselves from a white mob—only to have the houses later burned to the ground. In the same month the national capital became for three days the stamping-ground of rioters who were massed and did their will in the streets about the government buildings. The Negro residence district was made a zone which white men entered at their peril. Chicago, Knoxville, Omaha, Charleston, Elaine—the roster of names is monotonously long; the casualty lists startling. Each disaster in which hate found a vent and more hate was born came upon all the country, except the community which suffered, as a strange and terrible phenomenon—so terrible a commentary on our civilization as to be forgotten almost as soon as it was past. Vaguely, it was attributed to Negro criminality, the quick spread of a brawl, or to "race hatred." Southern editors jibed at Northern cities, and the North became aware of a "national problem." Awareness of that problem was intensified not so much by reason of the persons who died or were maimed as by the hatred displayed. It overran civil government and released primitive impulses in acts more bestial than the best or worst of savagery.

Cynics as to democratic processes remark by way of comment that in the cycle of history the crowd that howled down the streets of Rome under the late emperors is akin to to-day's mob—that empire let blood in the circus, and now democracy turns its streets into a Colosseum. It is an easy way of disposing of the race question to tell the individual that the kingdom of God is within him and that governments are only protean mobs. In its counsel of despair, it parallels the assertion of the amateur biologist who insists that Negro and white can never live peaceably side by side. Race relations must continue a hopeless problem, is the argument, for there is an "instinct" of race hatred; when a man's color or physiognomy is exceeding strange to you, you must necessarily hate him. The instinct is asserted to be a counterpart to the tendency of races to protect their "racial integrity." In so far as American race riots are concerned, the "instinct" of race hatred can be shown to be a fiction. The evidence from the race riots themselves, which have been caused by every sort of industrial and political conflict utterly unconnected with race relations, is borne out by the testimony of anthropologists, especially and chiefly Franz Boas.

Race riots, it will be shown, are attributable to nothing so simple as an instinct or a tendency. It is true that the passion which fighting-men feel is individual, but the determinants of that passion are environmental and social and are subject to control. The South, which created additional problems for the War Department by reason of its hostility to the presence and the training of Negro troops, held it against French people that they welcomed those troops. That is a commentary on the relation of environment to the "instinct" of race hatred. What is summarized as an instinct is rather a complex of the forces at work in the nation. Few aspects of American life, industrial, political, social, but are in some way contributory to the spirit which finds its release in mob clashes. Sometimes, lurking behind the name of race riot is discovered the plotting and counter-plotting of factions in a city government; almost always the evil spirit of propaganda; frequently, a contest between organized labor and employer; again, the activities of real-estate speculators. If government in this country is not to be relegated to hazardous intervals between mob impacts, the stimulants of race riots deserve examination and analysis.

The background for race riots is furnished by what might be called the "color psychosis" of the South. It is in the South that the problem of the adjustment of white and Negro populations has been rooted, and the South suffers from a chronic illness that is the consequence of the attitude of most Southern white men toward the Negro.

"Is the Negro out of politics in the South?"

asked Dr. W. E. B. DuBois some years ago. "Has there been a single Southern campaign in the last twenty years in which the Negro has not figured as the prime issue?" The penalty for the social and political disabilities imposed upon the Negro has been that he is constantly in the minds of white people. From contempt, with its admixture of self-reproach, to hostility is a short step and an easy one. Hence the apprehension with which the white South looked upon the induction of Negroes into the army; hence, in the past, the quick resort to the rope, the pistol, the torch. That the South is a "white man's country" is a dogma affirmed in practice not only oratorically and by editors, but with bullets and whip. It is expressed in lynchings and beatings, until the spirit of the Negro begins to change and he buys arms to defend himself. Then you have Longview, with white men dead and Negro residences burned.

The Southern dogma colors the opinions of the rest of the country. Negroes' houses were bombed in Chicago before the race riots of July, 1919. It is true that the influx of Negroes had caused real-estate values at first to become depreciated. But the bombings would never have taken place if the Negro himself, as a human being, had not been depreciated in the esteem of his neighbors by a hostile propaganda. Mr. Carl Sandburg[1] remarked that the Chicago police were inclined to believe the bombings the result rather of the "clash between two real-estate interests" than of "race feeling." If the diagnosis was correct it stands as another demonstration of the play of other motives on the relations of the races.

That the traditional attitude of the South has not been without effect was demonstrated in the Washington riots and in Omaha, where the mob outburst was not properly a race riot at all. In Washington, a propaganda conducted by several powerful newspapers, playing upon the sex antagonism of white men for black and accusing Negroes of assaults upon white women, inflamed hoodlums. In Omaha a similar propaganda undertaken from political motives brought about the lynching of a Negro suspect, the wrecking of the courthouse, and an attempt upon the life of the mayor. The propaganda of a particular Western newspaper was credited by the chief

[1] Carl Sandburg, *The Chicago Race Riots*, 1919. New York Harcourt, Brace & Howe.

of police, the Omaha Ministerial Union, and indirectly by Maj.-Gen. Leonard Wood with contributing to, if not causing, the riot; and it was established in court that the managing editor of that newspaper had been born and bred in the South. Reports of both Washington and Omaha riots sent to Northern newspapers assumed acquiescence in the Southern doctrine that the Negro is a rapist. Given the background of belief and superstition about the Negro which emanates from the South, it is not difficult to foment antagonisms.

Of the Chicago riot which followed hard upon Washington, no one even hinted that assaults by Negroes were a cause. As Mr. Sandburg pointed out, a multiplicity of elements brought about the tension which burst into violent conflict. But the main determinants here were (1) encroachments of migrant Negroes from the South upon white residence districts; (2) antagonism to non-union Negro workmen in the stockyards; (3) hostility arising from the part played by the Negro vote in electing an unpopular city administration. No insignificant part in fomenting race hatred in Chicago was played by the Kenwood and Hyde Park Property

Owners' Association. Months, even, after the riots, in which thirty-eight persons were killed, this association was sending out appeals to "every white person, property-owner in Hyde Park" to "protect your property." "Shall we sacrifice our property for a third of its value and run like rats from a burning ship," said a notice, "or shall we put up a united front and keep Hyde Park desirable for ourselves?" And a letter sent out at the same time said, "We are a red-blood organization who say openly, we won't be driven out." It is worthy of mention here that of two white men arrested in Chicago charged with bombing houses of Negroes and granted several extensions in court, one was a clerk in a real-estate concern. So obviously a cause of the Chicago violence was the antagonism to the expansion of the Negro residence district by migrants from the South, that the coroner proposed voluntary segregation of the races in his report on the riots.

Although municipal politics played their part in Chicago, the Omaha riot was most definitely and clearly inspired by antagonists of the city administration. Months before the lynching of William Brown, the local branch of the National Association for the Advancement of Colored People publicly called attention to the danger of the campaign conducted by this Western newspaper under its Southern editor. Every possible change was rung upon police inefficiency, and a main item in the campaign were alarmist reports of unpunished attacks of Negroes upon white women. The chief of police of Omaha, in a public statement, spoke of the "direct cause of riot" as being "the crystallization of mob spirit by vicious, unprincipled, and false newspaper criticisms of the police department." He added that the lynching party which stormed the jail "was quickly joined by a large number of local gamblers, bootleggers, auto thieves, and other criminals, brought to the scene of the riot in taxis, furnished with liquor, and urged to acts of lawlessness of every description by the 'gang,' in hope that the present city administration (note that they tried to hang the mayor) might be overthrown and handed over to their organization." "If the police administration is impotent to do its work," he asks later, "why have those who live on the vices of unfortunate women been so active in opposing the police department?"

Major-General Wood, who was put in command of the federal troops called to Omaha, remarked, pointedly: "One of the first steps toward the preservation of law and order should be the suppression of a rotten press, where there is one. I am strong for the freedom of the press where it is honest and fearless, gives facts and not lies. Free speech, yes, but not free treason." And on another occasion General Wood said, "With the exception of a few men and one paper, you have a good city."

Into the question whether the Omaha police department was or was not inefficient it is not at present necessary to go further than to say that the Omaha grand jury commented adversely on the conduct of the police forces during the strike. In any case, at the bottom of the Omaha lynching and of the riot which was diverted into attacks on unoffending colored men going about their business in the streets, was an embittered political controversy, having no connection with race and race hatred. Race hatred supplied the pretext upon which the political contest was brought violently to a focus.

The part played by the Western newspaper and the Southern newspapers in fanning passion to a dangerous point recalls Atlanta, and the newspaper which, according to Prof. Albert Bushnell Hart, "by its lurid statement of facts, large admixture of lies, and use of ferocious head-lines, was one of the chief agents in bringing about the Atlanta riots of 1907."[1]

Once conceded that the Negro may be a decisive element in local politics—Chicago's second ward, chiefly colored, having determined the election of Mayor Thompson—it is obvious that feeling with regard to the Negro will be played upon by the press. Unfortunately, even the routine of the press associations and of the important dailies gives an alarmist tinge to news accounts concerning the Negro. It is a commonplace that his crimes and not his achievements are reported. Dean Pickens, of Morgan College, has made the point that if the complexion of red-haired men were invariably mentioned in head-lines in connection with crimes they committed, small boys would run from the red-haired as though from a nightmare. The presumption in the white press is almost invariably against the Negro. When feeling becomes tense, as it was in Washington or

[1] Albert Bushnell Hart, *The Southern South*, p. 70.

Chicago, even a slight exaggeration in the reports of crimes committed by Negroes, an increased emphasis upon the race of the offender, at once attracts attention. A deliberate newspaper campaign to discredit the Negro cannot, under the circumstances, fail of dangerous success. Every such campaign is caught up and finds its echo in the colored and the white press throughout the country.

What is known as "tension"—a state of the public mind among colored and white people distinctly perceptible, but not easily described—increased at the time of the riots in other cities than the riot centers. If there had been a disposition to bring about a clash between colored and white people, in New York City, let us say, the best time for the attempt would have been immediately after the Chicago troubles, early in August, 1919.

A third determinant of race riots, besides political intrigue and the allied arts of the press, is the conflict between white union labor and unorganized Negroes. This was made clear in Chicago also, where the return of Negro workers to the stockyards had to be delayed after the riots had been stilled, because of the hostility of white workers. In fact, for months after the riots small racial disturbances did occur. Officers of the Stockyards Labor Council have denied harboring hostility to the Negro as Negro, and said they objected only to the presence of non-union men, Negro or white. In point of fact, the Negro has been and still is distrustful of unions. Too often he has had to go on strike only to find, when the time of settlement came, that the position he had left at the behest of his white comrades was filled by a white unionist. Throughout the South few Negroes are organized, and the Negro migrant carried his distrust of unions north with him.

The entrance of some 50,000 Negroes into Chicago industry, then, was of itself enough to create tension. A careful estimate by the National League on Urban Conditions Among Negroes of the number placed there since the migration gave 40,000 men and 12,000 women. Thus, in the fall of 1919 the stockyards were employing some 8,000 Negroes; the Corn Products Refining Company had increased the number of the Negro employees from 30 to 800 in a year, and various foundries and car companies each employed from 200 to 500 Negroes. Numbers of establishments, according to the Urban League, endeavored to maintain a ratio among their employees of three whites to one Negro, whereas the ratio of Negroes to the population was as one to thirty. In consequence many of those establishments ran foul of white unions and the Negro became a victim of the resulting hostility. During the steel strike numbers of Negroes were "imported," as immigrants used to be induced to come to our industrial centers to underbid union labor. In Pittsburgh it was estimated that 12,000 Negroes had been added to the labor supply. A story is told of the introduction of Negroes during the steel strike in one plant where they had not previously manned blast-furnaces. Confronted with the danger that the fires would go out, an officer of the company went to a Negro boarding-house and asked for twenty-five volunteers who thought they could operate the furnaces. He obtained the men, who were concealed in an engine-tender and driven to the mill. They kept the blast-furnaces going. Had the union enlisted their loyalty as the company was able to, the Negroes could not have been made an instrument for strike-breaking. For the Negro is no more a strike-breaker by nature than is the Czecho-Slovak or the Ukrainian.

Of late, as the industrial struggle has centered not so much about wages as about the right to organize and the maintenance of the closed shop, inducements offered to Negroes have often become such as to make them content to forgo the advantages of unionization. This condition played its part in Chicago and was accountable for the fury of the Irish-American stockyard workers adjacent to Chicago's "black belt." In this respect the Chicago riots resembled in type the East St. Louis massacre of 1917. Here, where six thousand Negroes were driven from their homes, and several hundred were hanged, shot, burned, or beaten, the importation by packing companies and other establishments of Negro strike-breakers directly contributed to the disaster. At the end of May, 1917, something over a month before the holocaust burst upon East St. Louis, six hundred union men, including striking employees of the Aluminum Ore Company, marched to the city hall to appeal against the importation of more Negroes, and these men were advised by the leaders, according to a correspondent of *The St. Louis Globe-Democrat*, "that in case the authorities took no action they should resort to mob law." The call to a meeting sent out by the Central Trades and Labor Union had spoken of the "influx of undesirable Negroes" and had said, "These men are being used to the detriment of our white citizens by some of the capitalists and a few of the real-estate owners." Of the sickening horrors that occurred during the massacres of East St. Louis it is unnecessary to speak, except to point out that the display of hatred and passion had its root in an industrial problem.

A very different set of industrial circumstances brought about the riots in Phillips County, Arkansas, in which some five white men and upward of twenty-five (some say more than one hundred) Negroes were killed. The Phillips County riots were widely heralded as the result of a "plot" on the part of Negroes to "massacre whites" and take over their land. Leadership in the "Negro insurrection" was variously attributed to Robert Hill, a Negro, to O. S. Bratton, a white man arrested on a charge of murder and subsequently released on his own recognizance under a purely formal indictment for "barratry" or fomenting litigation, and to "The Progressive Farmers and Household Union of America," an organization of Negro farmers of

Phillips County, Arkansas. Alarmist reports that fifty thousand rounds of ammunition had been found at a Negro school were later, less conspicuously, corrected when the principal explained they had been sent there for the military training of the students and had no connection whatever with the "insurrection." Investigation disclosed that the price of cotton and the farm-tenant system characteristic not only of Phillips County, Arkansas, but of the entire Southern cotton belt, had played an important part in the Phillips County troubles. The conduct of the proceedings against the accused Negro farm tenants bore out charges of oppression. Although feeling in Phillips County was such that no fair trial could possibly have been held there, they were tried and convicted by a jury from which Negroes had been excluded. A dozen Negroes were sentenced to be electrocuted and more than sixty to terms of from one to twenty-one years in prison. As against these sentences it will be recalled that many more Negroes, at least five Negroes for every white man, had been killed in the riots. The situation was given an entirely different color from the atmosphere of "massacre" and "insurrection" created by the press when U. S. Bratton, white native of Arkansas and member of a law firm of Little Rock, published his statement. He asserted that settlements, statements of their accounts, had been denied to the Negro tenants, who invariably found themselves in debt to their landlords at the end of the year; that a debt system, amounting virtually to peonage, had led the Negroes to organize and employ a lawyer to obtain legal redress; and that the riots as well as the court proceedings were designed to terrorize the Negro farm tenants out of asking for what was their due.

Mr. Bratton had been an Assistant United States Attorney and had vigorously prosecuted cases of peonage in that part of the state of Arkansas. This summary of the clashes about Elaine, Arkansas, is necessarily brief. It will be amplified later. But the bare facts sufficiently indicate that despite all romantic accounts of "Negro Paul Reveres" and their "night riding"—an absurdity to any one who knows the conditions in Arkansas and in the cotton-raising South—the price of cotton, land tenure, the system of plantation stores—all played their part in bringing on the Arkansas riots.

It will be seen that powerful social and

economic motives were operative in Chicago, Omaha, East St. Louis, Arkansas, Washington. It is to be assumed that riots so varied in their character suggest the variety of motive that plays about race antagonism. And yet the thought that arises, frequently unspoken, to people's minds in connection with race disturbances is sex. The riots in Washington were universally attributed to "many attacks upon white women" by Negroes; the victim of the Omaha mob, which then tried to hang the mayor, was a Negro accused of assault upon a white woman; the storming of the jail in Knoxville, preceding as it did general pillage and hoodlumism, had for its pretext the determination to lynch Maurice Mays, a Negro accused of assault. Of all preconceptions the one which fastens sexual crime to Negroes and unfailingly reverts to it in time of race conflict is most difficult to dispose of. The ground of misinformation is so firmly laid by a press whose campaign is based upon it that there is no hope of reaching newspaper readers with the facts. In effect, the mob spirit excited by news of sexual crime differs in no essential from the mobbism which finds expression in public hangings and burnings at stake in the Southern states. The public attitude toward race conflicts is deeply affected by the constant assertions of Southerners that lynching occurs for "one crime and one crime only"; so much so that it is found expedient, where a Negro man and a white woman have transgressed the Southern code, and the Negro has paid for it with his life, to accuse the Negro of having committed assault. The fact remains that, despite the propaganda which justifies mob murder of Negroes on the ground of the protection of white womanhood, sex antagonism was not the occasion of most of the race riots in this country. Sex jealousy has been used and exploited to foment hatred. Individual mobbists have undoubtedly been moved by the passion of sex jealousy fostered not only by the newspapers, but by the utterances of Senators and Representatives in the national Capitol. To that extent the motives of the individual and of groups of the population may be roused, stimulated, used in the plans and purposes of political or business or labor leaders. It is hardly necessary to advert to the type of agitation conducted by a well-known Southern ex-Senator. Professor Hart has spoken of the "genius of Benjamin R.

Tillman in discovering that there are more voters of the lower class than of the upper, and that he who can get the lower class to vote together may always be re-elected." Although, Professor Hart added, Tillman came of a respectable middle-class family, yet it was his part "to show himself the coarsest and most vituperative of poor whites." It is a type of leadership still prevalent, still vocal in the Senate and House of Representatives, still effective in newspaper offices and from the platform in inflaming men to the point where mob conflict between the races becomes possible. Its theme is often social equality, and great pains are taken to confuse the public mind by identifying social equality with race mixture.

If the white man is deluded by the talk about sex and Negro criminality, the Negro is not. Especially clear is the Negro bourgeoisie, a group unknown to most white people because it is part of what Doctor DuBois has called the "group economy" of race in this country. "It consists," said Doctor DuBois, "of a co-operative arrangement of industry and service in a group which tends to make the group a closed economic circle, largely independent of surrounding whites.

. . . The Negro lawyer serves almost exclusively colored clientage, so that his existence is half forgotten by the white world."

A rough measure of the present power and importance of the Negro bourgeoisie is in the scope of its financial enterprises, its life-insurance companies, banking institutions, lodges, farms, residences, oil-wells. There is not space to speak of Negro colleges and schools, of the achievements of Negro lawyers and physicians and dentists, many of whom enjoy the best white patronage. The existence of the Negro bourgeoisie, however, should be borne in mind as a determinant of the changed status of the Negro in the United States and of the Negro's changed attitude toward race conflict. With the exception of Arkansas, where the rural Negro was more or less at the mercy of the better armed and better organized white man, recent race riots have not been massacres. The Negro has shot to kill, to defend himself, and in a number of cases it was this circumstance as much as the activity of local police or the intervention of troops which put an end to disorder.

It would be exaggeration to ascribe to the war the development of the "new Negro."

Fifty years of such progress as has been accomplished by the Negro race in this country were bound to produce more and more individuals who would bitterly resent the disabilities imposed on them merely and only on the pretext of the color of their skins and by reason of the blind prejudices of white men. Knowing, as Negroes bitterly have come to know, that vengeance is visited upon those of their race who advance materially, that it is not the Negro servant, but the Negro landowner, teacher, physician, who bears the brunt of race prejudice, that, in short, it is class and not race prejudice, that poisons race relations, Negroes were bound to develop race consciousness. This development went hand in hand with the economic "group economy" which Doctor DuBois has described. If the white press omits essential interpretations of race phenomena, the Negro press of this country does not. White men were amazed in Civil War times at the rapid dissemination of news by the "grapevine" system of communication among Negroes. Now, even where colored men are terrorized out of distributing or buying their newspapers and magazines, such as *The Chicago Defender*, with its large circulation, *The Crisis*,

The Messenger, The New York Age, news spreads from those who do succeed in obtaining and reading these and many other publications of the race. The function of the war, of the better jobs, higher cotton prices, and opportunity in the North which it brought, was not to create Negro leaders, business men, a class of intelligent and responsible citizens. They had come into being before the war. They represented all the social stratification of a highly developed capitalist state with their own means of communication, of finance, and instruments of industry. What the war taught Negroes anew was that they must stand together on the basis of color. That the hard reminders had had their effect was demonstrated in the race clashes of 1919. Substantial Negroes, who had hoped to keep aloof from the inevitable clashes of hoodlums, found themselves forced to buy rifles and ammunition. They found themselves victimized by the reports given currency by politicians like Vardaman, that "Frenchwomen-ruined niggers" were coming back to this country from France to make trouble and to disturb the supremacy of the white race. More than one such Negro, with business responsibilities and a family that would have disposed him to peace, had peace been possible, had to consider fighting for his manhood, not with the ballot, but with the gun. That Negroes were insulted for no other reason than that they wore the uniform of the United States army, when on the one hand they were being taught to value democracy, and on the other hand were being taught to fight, could not fail to have its effect upon the attitude of the Negro toward the white mob.

In effect, race riots represent a repudiation of civilization on the part of the group which initiates and tolerates them, as preferable to the tolerance on terms of equality of another group in that civilization. So long as the relations of Negro and white man in this country are conceived in the terms of the black man's encroachment upon the white man's sexual preserve there will be embittered hostility between the races. When the term "social equality" is divested of its special significance and is used literally to mean equal treatment for human beings on the basis of their common humanity, a long step will have been taken toward the elimination of the rope, the torch, and the gun from American government. When that new use of the term "social equality" has been initiated, it will be understood that, as Mr. Walter Lippmann has put it, we can give the Negro complete access to all the machinery of our common civilization and "allow him to live so that no Negro need dream of a white heaven and of bleached angels."

For the present, race riots and armed watching and waiting between the colored and white men in American cities show the soft and the rotten spots in our civilization. They show a press undisciplined to any sense of social responsibility; freedom not for the social inventor, but for the exploiter who plays his own tunes on passion; dark centers of poverty and crime which become the source of disorder that involves the best of both races in hostility and embittered misunderstanding.

The way out is not to disarm the Negro and subject him to terrorism. That makes jailers and tyrants of white Americans. "They won't sell us arms, but I notice they still sell us kerosene," was the remark of one colored man. To allow a race to advance economically and socially, even against such obstacles as have confronted the Negro, and to tell him to remain a hewer of wood and a drawer of water is not only to run counter to the American tradition, but it is to set one's face toward achieving the impossible.

Race riots have shown, as no other phenomenon of race relations in the United States, the complexity and variety of problems that confront democracy. More and more it is coming to be realized that the Negro is demanding a new orientation in the United States. The road to that orientation lies through education, improved housing and sanitation, increased opportunity. To permit the manifestation on the part of white men of distaste or hostility to a colored skin to determine the approach to race relations, or to permit an embittered assertion of class superiority, with skin pigmentation as its distinguishing mark, is to court the anarchy and the savagery that prevail when dark men gather armed in their districts to repel the white mob and white mobs wander the streets, beating to insensibility or death any colored man who chances to be in their way. More than any agency in the country the press can contribute to the elimination of race riots. For the present, local government is ineffective to prevent armed clashes. Usually, when that stage has been reached, the assistance of the federal government and the intervention of either state or federal troops has to be invoked. Race riots are the confession of democracy's failure to deal with one of the main problems of the modern world—"the color line," the relation of men of widely different races. Ultimately the problem must be attacked and solved within nations. For no nation is a homogeneous racial entity. The discipline of tolerance will be found a necessary step in the maintenance of international relations. To permit the enmities of the races of the world to be embodied in miniature within the boundaries of the United States is to allow a menace to grow of the ruin of civilization as we conceive it.

It should be said of the present tension, with its outbursts of race conflicts, that it presents encouraging aspects. The Negro has a stake in American civilization and he is willing to fight for it. Of the quality of life and of freedom the hard lesson is being learned more deeply by the Negro than by any class in America. Truly for many Negroes life and freedom are a daily conquest. The patience and determination and courage which go into the struggle are values that no nation can afford to spurn. Something of respect for an adversary who stands his ground is admixed with the shame and regret of white communities, like Washington, which have tolerated riot. If the result of race riots is, as some observers profess to see it, a new standing and a new recognition of the Negro, as well as a new realization and race pride on the part of Negroes themselves, the price of lives lost and suffering will not have been exacted altogether in vain.

III

THE SOUTH'S COLOR PSYCHOSIS

TO Europeans and to many Northerners the attitude of the Southerner toward the Negro is a feast of unreason. Why will a Southerner of caste refer affectionately to the colored mammy who rocked him to sleep on her bosom, who told him the stories that colored the dawning of the world upon his mind? Why will the same gentleman regard it as an insult to be asked to ride in a Pullman car with that mammy's son? Why must the colored boy, who has played with little white children, pass them in the street later with scarcely a nod of recognition from them? Why is it possible, at the mere mention of "social equality" of the races, to rouse such fury among Southern white people that many a colored man has paid with his life the unsupported accusation of having "preached" that equality? To attempt to answer these and similar questions offhand is to disregard the simple fact that a set of beliefs, which are emotionally unified and harmonized in the person who holds them, often seem extravagantly incompatible and illogical to the critical observer. Unfortunately for the South, as well as for the nation, the consequence of the typical attitude toward race relations is not merely an effect of illogicality upon the observer. The effect is the continuance in the South of a state of feeling closely akin to the hysteria which swept the rest of the nation in the time of the World War.

The Southern white man puts certain questions beyond the bounds of discussion. If they are pressed he will fight rather than argue. What to many educated and cultivated persons of the North seems arguable and debatable, subject to critical examination and referable to scientific observation, to the Southern white man is as sacred as religious dogma and is defended as passionately. In matters of social and political concern, then, many Southern white men, not excluding Senators and editors of the most powerful newspapers, act upon beliefs as rigid and apparently unalterable as those which animated the hunters of schismatics and heretics in the early Christian Church and during the Middle Ages. To such minds any attempt to swerve or convince them is a sort of treason; differences of opinion, like differences in faith, are subject to the arbitrament of force. The state of mind, common as it is to all classes, with whatever exceptions every class affords, determines, within the limits of the federal constitution, the laws of Southern states, the enforcement of those laws, and all the subtleties of human relations which are not reflected in court cases. The result is not a stable human society, but a balance of power. Where men may not publicly express dissent unless in fear of ostracism, where social standing and, in many communities, tolerable existence depend upon very definitely prescribed orthodoxy, it is not assent, but power that determines the continuance of a social and industrial system based on that orthodoxy. The question of the Negro's status in the South is quite generally disposed of by the assertion that the South is a "white man's country" and must remain so. The position cannot be justified on grounds of any general political or social principles applicable to human beings in general, without either specifically excepting the Negro as a class from the application of those principles or declaring that he is not a human being. In practice both expedients are resorted to.

But the Negro, where he acquires economic power, farms, Liberty bonds, oil-wells, theaters, education, medical and legal training, constantly narrows the field which may be interposed between himself and common humanity. It is very difficult to show that the man is not a human being who can administer a three-thousand-acre farm; who can represent the United States as consul—with diplomatic responsibilities—in Latin America; who can perform difficult and delicate surgical operations; who writes poetry and music, conducts banks and life-insurance companies. When this denial of power becomes a *reductio ad absurdum* on the basis of any test of ability or aptitude which may be advanced, the recourse is always to something inherent in color. Every successful colored man, then, becomes living disproof of the 100-per-cent. Southerner's theorem.

The symptoms of the South's state of mind are forms of repression which the North would resort to only under the threat of war and toward enemies or those believed to be sympathizing with and aiding the enemy.[1] There is no crime so heinous that it puts the offender in civilized communities outside the field of court procedure. In almost all countries pretending to civilization the accused is entitled, as a matter of course, to trial to determine if he be guilty or not. That is not the case in many portions of the South. Public men, where they do not participate in the mob murder without trial of colored men, frequently condone or approve it. It is not uncommon for a newspaper editorial to urge that the exponent of an unpopular doctrine be "lynched." Where else than in the Southern states of the United States would it be possible to remove a man from a railway train and beat him within an inch of his life because, being colored, he had dared to purchase Pullman accommodations for his two daughters, on their journey to a Southern university of standing? To all questions that may be raised as to the propriety of using force and threats of it in administering race relations, the reply is that by that means they are "settled." The

[1] This statement becomes theoretical since the hysterical outburst of radical baiting and hunting of "Reds" which took place in Northern cities late in 1919 and early in 1920.

answer leaves much to be desired. The "settlement" is accompanied by serious disadvantages. Uneasy lies the Southerner's head whose ascendancy, like the king's, depends upon repression. He is tied to a slavery worse almost than physical enslavement. His thoughts and preoccupations are chained to color and the problems race relations occasion. In commenting upon the riots at Vicksburg in 1874, Garner speaks of "the dread of Negro insurrection, which has at one time or another darkened every hearthstone in the South"; rumors of uprising, massacre, plotting by Negroes, appeared in many newspapers during 1919, created intense anxiety, and provoked violent countermeasures. Agrarian and almost entirely economic as the origin of the disturbances in Arkansas proved to have been, the newspapers not only of the South, but throughout the nation, reflected the fear of revolt, massacre, and uprising which is never blotted entirely out of the mind of the white citizens of the South.

Something more than analogy is possible between what the nation had to believe of the individual German when it was fighting Germany and what the South habitually believes of the Negro. It is difficult to generate enough enthusiasm to fight a man unless you hate him; and it is difficult to hate him unless you believe him better, in some respects, than yourself and are jealous, or conceive him utterly unworthy of human consideration, a beast, degenerate, criminal. In neither case are you in a position to discuss any questions which may be raised as to your relations to the individual. He is enemy, and hate or contempt is justified in wreaking itself upon him and upon his protagonists. Many Southerners protest they have intense and sympathetic affection for individual Negroes such as is not found elsewhere in the United States. That may or may not be true of certain individuals. But let the Negro insist, not upon affectionate condescension, but upon his full prerogatives as a man and a citizen of the United States, and his most devoted Southern friends will relegate him to the position the "Hun" occupied during the war.

That this condition of the public mind is due not to something inherent in race there are numerous indications. "No people," says Bryce, "was ever prouder than the Romans, nor with better reason. Yet, though in the fullness of their strength they held themselves called by Fate to rule the world, they showed little contempt for their provincial subjects and no racial aversion."[1] In the ancient world, dark skin, as Bryce points out, excited little or no repulsion. His valuable survey suggests to him "that down till the days of the French Revolution there had been very little in any country, or at any time, of self-conscious racial feeling." In those countries where race hatred has been thought to be most active as a motive, Bryce has shown the play of other forces: in Hungary and Transylvania it was "not till some time after the Napoleonic wars" that there began to be "talk of antagonism between Magyars, whether nobles or peasants, and the subject Slavs or Rumans." It is nevertheless a matter of record that the Magyar conceived the Slovaks as being not human. In Bohemia the quarrels of Czechs with the smaller German element "were not purely racial, but complicated with the religious disputes of the Hussites and the orthodox Catholics, and with scholastic disputes between the Nominalists (mostly Germans)

[1] Viscount Bryce, "Race Sentiment as a Factor in History." A lecture delivered before the University of London, February 22, 1915.

and the Realist party, which embraced the bulk of Czech teachers and students." As regards Ireland, "the sentiment of a separate Irish nationality seems to date from the strife, first over land and then over religion also, which began in the time of Elizabeth." Yet although national feeling, "even in the days of the United Irishmen and the rebellion of 1798 . . . was not distinctively racial," it was treated as such by those Englishmen who proved that the Irish were inferior. Even to-day in the Western Hemisphere the very Negro who, it is believed by so many white Americans, occasions insurmountable obstacles to the maintenance of civilization, is absorbed and assimilated. In Brazil, whose Negro population is most numerous of the Latin-American republics, there is no race feeling against intermarriage. Persons of mixed blood are considered white and augment the white population. "The result is so far satisfactory," says Bryce, "that there is little or no class friction. The white man does not lynch or maltreat the Negro; indeed, I have never heard of a lynching anywhere in South America except occasionally as part of a political convulsion. The Negro is not accused of insolence and does not seem to develop any more criminality than naturally belongs to any ignorant population with loose notions of morality and property."[1]

Three conclusions are suggested by Bryce from his South American observations, of which two are especially pertinent: The first that a race, the result of fusion of two parent stocks, is not necessarily inferior to the stronger parent or superior to the weaker; the second that "race repugnance is no such constant and permanent factor in human affairs as members of the Teutonic peoples are apt to assume. Instead of being, as we Teutons suppose, the rule in this matter, we are rather the exception," and history as well as observation of our world seems to suggest "that since the phenomenon is not of the essence of human nature, it may not be always so strong among the Teutonic peoples as it is to-day."

The exceptional phenomenon, then, which invidiously distinguishes white Americans from Mohammedans, Chinese, the Latin races, is referable to something not essentially different from Jewish pride. If the Jew was born to teach, the Anglo-Saxon was born to rule.

[1] James Bryce, *South America*, 1912. New York: The Macmillan Company. P. 480.

On the blood of the Jew a religious inheritance had set a high price; on the blood of the Anglo-Saxon a political tradition of far more recent date, due in large measure to Norman heritage. Every race so distinguished, not biologically, but by its own cult of superiority, by its traditions and its self-interpretation, becomes to that degree an only child of God, spoiled and hated. Science has not meant the extinction of God; but it has sounded the doom of tribal and racial gods. And in science's twilight of the gods lurks the promise of a brighter dawn in which races will be valued not by any scale of superior or inferior, quantitatively, but as different colors in civilization, qualitatively different.

If the effect of the Southerner's assumptions is to make him believe the Negro to be racially inferior, he must resent proof to the contrary. It is proper for an inferior race to serve, to hew wood and draw water, to pick cotton, to work the farm. It is a reversal of the divine plan for the inferior to aspire to the seats of the mighty, to want to become postmasters in Southern towns, or aldermen. The divine plan is, like most plans, subject to interpretation. It precludes voting for Negroes south of the Ohio River in the opinion of some. But

Atlanta, Georgia, is south of the Ohio River and Negroes of Atlanta vote for President of the United States. In 1919 the Negroes of Atlanta defeated at the polls a proposal to issue bonds because the white citizens had not agreed to equitable expenditure of the proceeds on Negro schools. This was also contrary to the divine plan.

The insistence on divine plan, on dogma, always implies a process of rationalization. The believer maintains his point of view with desperate insistence, not by accumulating facts and reasoning from them. That process, the result of idle curiosity and dispassionate investigation, deals death to dogma. But rationalization is the process of interpreting the facts with reference to beliefs arrived at before the facts are examined. That is what poisons race relations in the South and in a measure affects the thinking of all Americans on the subject. The dogmatist on the subject of race inferiority not only resists reasoning, he resists fact. The despised literary gentlemen of the North, sometimes known as "nigger-lovers," discuss the undebatable, or, as a Negro preacher once put it, unscrew the inscrutable.

What are typical Southern attitudes toward

the race question? There are many, and a statement of each would be emphatically repudiated by a large part of the population to which it was attributed. The cultivated Southern gentleman of the middle-class family which knows Negroes chiefly as house servants, as tradesmen, or even as artisans would dissent from the expressions used by the poor white. Historically the relations between the Negro and the ruling classes of the South have often been closer than those between the Southerner of lineage and culture and the poor white. In fact, the colored man, by the account of one of his own spokesmen, who acted as Speaker of the Mississippi legislature during Reconstruction days, preferred the aristocrat of the past. Even during slavery days their relations had been cordial and friendly. Women of the best white families had taught and cared for slaves, had conducted religious services, and had maintained personal relations which were regarded as their duty and were their pride. Where the white aristocrat had sometimes harbored a tolerance which came of affectionate condescension and was reinforced by a realization of the material advantages of the enforced associations, the poor white felt antipathy and jealousy. The Negro, in his eyes, was an instrument of oppression, a competitor in the industrial market, whose function it was to undercut the white artisan's wages and to degrade him. It was not long after the introduction of slaves before plantation-owners learned that Negro slaves could be used as carpenters, shoemakers, plasterers, painters, blacksmiths, drivers of teams. "Although the slaves were not responsible for this condition," says Lynch, "the fact that they were there and were thus utilized created a feeling of bitterness and antipathy on the part of the laboring whites which could not be easily wiped out."[1]

The growth of large plantations, the relegation of the poor white to less fertile areas, the same conditions which have always militated against immigration of foreigners to the South on any appreciable scale, have contrived to keep this animosity alive. The poor white had this much compensation, however: "A white man was always a white man," as Prof. Albert Bushnell Hart points out, "and as long as slavery endured, the poorest and most ignorant of the white race

[1] John R. Lynch, *The Facts of Reconstruction*, 1915. New York: Neale Publishing Co. P. 108.

could always feel that he had something to look down upon, that he belonged to the lords of the soil. In the war he was blindly and unconsciously fighting for the caste of white men, and could not be brought to realize that slavery helped to keep him where he was, without education for his children, without opportunities for employment, without that ambition for white paint and green blinds which has done so much to raise the Northern settler."[1]

The Civil War has been aptly called a rich man's war and a poor man's fight. The motives, then, for antagonism between poor white and Negro have been among the most powerful common to human beings—jealousy and pride. In industry the white artisan hated the Negro as a favored competitor. This hatred was bound to find expression in the fields in which the white man was favored—the political and social. It was a form of compensation that, poor as the white might be, he was yet kin with the owner and master of slaves, could afford to despise and insult the black man. Strange as it may seem, on the ground that they were extravagantly administered and meant heavy taxa-

[1] *The Southern South*, p 40.

tion—surely no sore burden on the poor whites as a class—the introduction of public schools during Reconstruction days met with the most determined opposition, even from the poor whites themselves, whose status the schools might have been expected to improve. Fifty or sixty years is a short space in which to change feelings so deeply ingrained as hatred for black men on the part of poor whites. Even yet it is operative and plays its part in preventing absorption of colored workmen in white unions, introducing new industrial problems and the hates and distrusts consequent upon mutual exclusiveness. The white man's feelings of superiority are still played upon for political profit and are linked, by processes which might be examined in detail, to the most powerful of man's impulses and emotions—those related to sex.

"The last fatal campaign in Georgia which culminated in the Atlanta massacre," says Doctor DuBois, "was an attempt, fathered by conscienceless politicians, to arouse the prejudices of the rank and file of white laborers and farmers against the growing competition of black men, so that black men by law could be forced back to subserviency and serfdom. It succeeded so well that smoldering hate burst into flaming murder before the politicians could curb it."

In the South, the chivalresque notions of human intercourse, with their picturesqueness and their disadvantages, survived longer than elsewhere in the United States. The beauties of the old régime are sometimes overdrawn, just as the historian of the court functions of the time of Louis XIV often forgets to describe the odors which, in the absence of sanitation, almost caused the stoutest ambassadors and perfumed, bewigged, buckled, and laced gentlemen to faint. Like any civilization whose eyes are blinded to the substructure of misery and desolation upon which it rests, its charms are canonized. The divine right of kings has never been affirmed with more certitude than the right of the white aristocrat of the South to rule and to profit from the enforced servitude of the black man. The chivalresque tradition which was exemplified in the ideal animating the aristocratic South no less than in the romances of medieval Europe emphasized not inquiry, service, labor such as is the badge of distinction among scientists. It rewarded personal prowess, sportsmanship, courtesy, and, in matters intellectual, conformity. Properly cultivated, the chivalresque tradition has much to give to this country, perhaps through such Southern gentlemen as preserve appreciation of values less temporal than those measurable by the dollar or by popular acclaim. But on the relations of the races the effect of the chivalresque traditions was almost uniformly bad. It led men to assert as permanent and immutable a system whose consequences they did not stop to examine. It transmuted to romance, faith, nobility, and a whole dictionary of appealing terms attitudes grounded in base pecuniary considerations. Toward any investigation into its own foundations it perpetuated an attitude of condemnation as toward sacrilege.

"Nothing was so prejudicial to slavery," says Professor Hart, "as the attempt to silence the Northern abolitionists; for a social system that was too fragile to be discussed was doomed to be broken."

It is too often assumed that the Civil War broke that system. It survives still, subject to a subtler process of disintegration than war, leaving its last records not only in memoirs and mellow reminiscences, but in blood, violence, terror, and hatred. Many Southern white men of the laboring classes deplore the industrial policy of *divide et impera*, which is used to exploit both them and colored men. So do many Southern white men of the possessing and industrial classes deplore the exploitation of the Negro politically and industrially. The attitude of these dissenters, however, is not typical of preponderant groups; and it is not vocal. An iron conformity is still clamped upon the South and holds to its standards him who would remain a part of its political, social, and industrial activities.

Before the Civil War white aristocrats were never put in any position in which they might be forced into competition with the Negro. Manual labor finds no place in a chivalresque tradition. It was the part of the white man to administer, to superintend, to plan. Further, manual labor was made a social criterion which even now, in more advanced civilizations, except in the case of the sculptor, painter, musician, and craftsman, divides the "upper" from the "lower" classes. To a degree the distinction survives in that the prejudice against the colored man is now directed against those who "rise" above the socially inferior laboring class. This social prejudice plays easily into the industrial need for a large supply of cheap labor.

"In the last analysis," remarks Professor Hart, "most of the objections to Negro education come down to the assertion that it puts the race above the calling whereunto God hath appointed it. The argument goes back to the unconscious presumption that the Negro was created to work the white man's field, and that even a little knowledge makes him ambitious to do something else."

There is even yet a large body of opinion in the South which would deny the Negro education, not only because ignorance makes him a source of exploitable labor, but because it debars him from participation in the prerogative of the superior race—ruling by political processes. When it was undreamed of that colored men might vote, participation was not a class distinction. As soon as the vote and office-holding became an issue, it became as sacred as a dogma that the Negro was unfit politically, as that industrially he was unfit for anything but the rougher and more arduous kinds of labor. But the economic advance of the Negro, the growth of a Negro bourgeoisie, has threatened these assumptions. With wealth and the advantages that wealth brings at his command, many a Negro threatens the white man's complacence. It is against the advancing, prosperous colored man, therefore, that fury is frequently directed. If a Negro, outside of the few large Southern cities, presumes to dress well, he is known as a "dude nigger." Many a Negro in large Southern cities, even, is confronted daily with signs informing him that dogs and Negroes are not permitted in the public parks, thus making it clear that, whatever his competency, education, and sensibilities, racial barriers are immutable.

"The whole South," remarks Professor Hart, "is full of evidence not so much that the whites think the Negroes inferior, as that they think it necessary to fix upon him some public evidence of inferiority, lest mistakes be made."

"It not infrequently happens," says the Department of Labor's report on Negro Migration in 1916–17, "that the Negro who obviously makes money and gets out of debt is dismissed from the plantation, a common expression being that as soon as a Negro begins to make money he is no longer of any account."

The evidence as to the humiliations to

which Negroes are subject in large cities of the South is so voluminous that it is hardly necessary to adduce it here. The quality of treatment accorded respectable colored people, however, is suggested in another passage from the Labor Department's report:

"Most of the larger Southern cities not only exclude Negroes from their fine parks, but make little or no provisions for the recreation of the colored people. Harassing, humiliating 'Jim-Crow' regulations surround Negroes on every hand and invite unnecessarily severe and annoying treatment from the public and even from public servants. To avoid trouble, interference, and even injury, Negroes must practise eternal vigilance in the streets and on common carriers. The possibilities of trouble are greatly increased if the colored men are accompanied by their wives, daughters, or sweethearts. For then they are more likely to resent violently any rough treatment or abuse, and insulting language, whether addressed directly to them or to the women. Colored women understand this so well that they frequently take up their own defense rather than expose their male friends to the danger of protecting them."

It will be appreciated to what extent

absolutist distinctions are made on the basis of color, fortified by traditional, industrial, and political considerations, when it is remembered that the chivalresque culture demands the protection of womanhood from violence, from insult, even, at the cost of life itself. Subject to forces of attrition, the white man's scheme of the South constitutes a closed system, intolerable to the manhood and womanhood—provided manhood and womanhood be conceded to them—of any individuals of whatever race who are subjected to it. Fortified as it is by dogma, exempt from examination or discussion, the imposition of it remains, as has been stated, a matter of *force majeure.* The nation is no longer divided against itself to the extent that it was before the Civil War. But the South is divided against itself to an extent known only to Southerners, especially Southern colored people. The World War, which might have been expected to override waves of dissent, to engulf in an emotional flood of national sentiment all but irreconcilable differences, intensified the strains and stresses which race feeling has imposed upon the social structure of the Southern states. The War Department encountered fierce resistance to the quartering of colored troops in Southern communities, in fact to the enlistment and training of colored men; although the draft boards, from which colored men were excluded, discriminated in the matter of exemptions and certifications against Negroes. The net effect upon white Americans of the service of Negroes in the armies of the United States was a dangerous increase in bitterness and resentment, a determination to "show the nigger" when he returned from service that the equality to some extent imposed by the United States government in its military arm was not to affect political or social relations when the emergency had passed.

A balance in any such social system is possible only when the victims of that system are thoroughly cowed. Meanwhile that balance is represented by peculiar phrases and attitudes not common to the rest of the country. Thus to be "radical" elsewhere than in the South has signified general political liberalism of a sort more or less extreme. In the South to be radical has meant to most people an intolerable attitude on race relations, to wit, a tendency to espouse the cause of the "nigger." The word "radical" took on its significance in Civil War and Reconstruction days. Because the board of trustees of a Mississippi educational institution included "carpet-baggers" and native Republicans, *The Jackson Clarion* voiced its abhorrence in these terms:

"The people have revolted at the thought of placing their sons under radical patronage, when the country abounds with schools uncorrupted by radical influences."[1]

Times have changed. Republicans elsewhere may be reactionary, stand-pat, conservative, or any shade between; but in many communities of the South to vote Republican is to "vote nigger" and be a dangerous or contemptible "radical," unworthy of association with decent people. It will readily be seen that thereby certain bounds are set to that flexibility of political discussion which is supposed to be characteristic of so experimental and undogmatic a form of government as democracy. Only the most thundering acceptance of current claptrap about Negro inferiority, the most obvious pandering to prejudice, hatred, and apprehension, will meet the public mind dominated by such obsessions as have been suggested. When the balance of that system is disturbed, because it is sus-

[1] Quoted by Garner, *op. cit.*, footnote p. 368.

pected that victims may resist, political discussion enters a more violent phase, in which all white men become a tribe massed and gathered to fight for its very existence. There are, of course, those who stand above and aside from the battle. But they are not elected to the Senate or the House of Representatives; they write few editorials.

Violence in the South is not only always imminent; it is actual. "Lawlessness," says Professor Hart—and hundreds of other observers will corroborate him—"is the plague of the South. . . . The number of homicides and mob murders is not so serious as the continual appeals to violence by editors and public men who are accepted as leaders by a large minority and sometimes a majority of the white people." "The commonest form of terror," he says later, "is lynching, a deliberate attempt to keep the race down by occasionally killing Negroes sometimes because they are dreadful criminals, frequently because they are bad, or loose-tongued, or influential, or are acquiring property, or otherwise irritate the whites." Many a white Southerner will confess in casual conversation that he believes it necessary to "lynch a nigger" now and then in order that they may be kept in their place; and what that place is in the white Southerner's estimation has been sufficiently indicated. Meanwhile the bonds of personal relationship which used to mitigate the hostility of races under slavery, when white aristocrat and colored people had points of contact, are steadily being dissolved. Testimony is almost unanimous to the effect that the gap between white people of standing and Negroes is being widened.

In Reconstruction days the white men and women who came from New England to teach in Negro schools were unable to obtain board or lodging in the homes of Southern white people and often had to live with Negroes. "Living upon terms of social equality with the Negroes was a grave offense in the eyes of the Southern white," says Garner, "and was sure to cost the offender whatever respect the community might otherwise have entertained for him."

Of the teachers who were whipped and the schools burned, of the teacher who was charged by the Ku-Klux with "associating with Negroes in preference to the white race as God ordained," the trace survives. Then it was deemed a disgrace for a woman to teach in a Negro school. It is a practice scarcely more honored now than it was, although the insult which accompanied has to some degree fallen away. But the breach between white and colored people remains and widens.

Of the colored man's attitude toward the social system of the South, the white man who "knows the nigger" is almost entirely ignorant. Few if any white men ever enter Negro homes; they do not attend Negro meetings or churches. They are not spoken to frankly, except by certain colored men who are terrorized or bribed into sycophancy. Few Negroes trust the Southern white man; and although their commerce may be amiable and peaceable, it is seldom the white man knows what the Negro is thinking. But the Negro knows the white man's thoughts. He knows because members of his race are in constant association with and attendance upon the whites; and, too, there are many Negroes of so light complexion that unless they are personally known they are indistinguishable from white men. That circumstance, in the event of tension and imminent violence, makes the maintenance of secrecy a matter of difficulty for the "superior" race.

It will be noticed that the discussion of race relations at this point becomes a consideration of a potential state of war. That condition becomes more and more a menace as the Negro advances, as he decides that he will fight and die rather than be lynched, Jim-Crowed, terrorized, browbeaten, and robbed. It was not until the migration reached its height and Southern plantations and farms were being seriously depleted of labor that a process of soul-searching began which found its echo even in editorials of the Negro's bitterest antagonists among the press. Said *The Daily News*, of Jackson, Mississippi:

"We allow petty officers of the law to harass and oppress our Negro labor, mulcting them of their wages, assessing stiff fines on trivial charges, and often they are convicted on charges which if preferred against a white man would result in prompt acquittal." [1]

The Charlotte Observer remarked that "the real thing that started the exodus lies at the door of the farmer and is easily within his power to remedy. The Negro must be given better homes and better surroundings. Fifty years after the Civil War he should not be expected to be content with the same con-

[1] Quoted in *Negro Migration in 1916–17*. U. S. Labor Department.

ditions which existed at the close of the war."[1]

The white South's first response to the migration was, as might have been expected, violent resentment. It is not much good being a superior race if the inferior race moves away. Doubtless the beginning of the northward movement was assisted by the ravages of the boll weevil in the Southwest. But the migration continued and grew and it was borne in upon the most unobservant that among the many motives which prompted Negroes to leave the South was a desire for educational opportunities for their children, for human and kindly intercourse, for citizenship and the vote. Blind as the nation had been to the failure of attempts to "settle" problems of race relations by violence and terrorism, murder and lynching, mitigated if at all by condescension, it could not disregard the evidence presented by the northward migration and by the imminence of armed violence in many Southern cities. When it is deemed necessary, in anticipation of the use of revolvers and guns, to stop selling them to Negroes, although the sale to whites goes on unchecked, it would seem the part of wisdom

[1] Quoted in *Negro Migration in 1916–17*. U. S. Labor Department.

to delve into the resentment which turns finally for redress not to courts, but to desperate self-defense. Conditions such as prevailed in 1919 were doubtless in part due to that vague diffusion of discontent and assertions after the war known as "unrest." But any such system as prevailed and as still prevails in the Southern states of the United States was bound to arrive at a point where readjustment, either by intelligent direction or in violent conflict, would be unavoidable.

It may be thought that the characterization of relations between the races in the South bears unduly upon the shortcomings of the Southern white man. In point of fact, it would be difficult to exaggerate the ignorance and brutality characteristic of many rural communities. There are, of course, vast numbers of middle-class and cultivated people very much like similar populations elsewhere. But they are perforce silent and acquiescent in the system of thought which is formed, as I have suggested, by inheritance, by economic and political considerations, and is made effectual not by the people who deplore excesses, but by the many who are wanting in civilized inhibitions. Rarely, unless by such a catastrophe as the Atlanta riots, is the better sentiment of citizens roused to the self-assertion which makes repetition of such horrors impossible. Even now there are persons who foresee progressive degeneration of good will among white and black men, not because elsewhere in the world there is lacking demonstration that a *modus vivendi* could be devised, but because most of the effective forces playing upon race relations at present, such as the press, public discussion, industrial policy, are contriving to intensify and make more malignant the disease of hatred and misunderstanding which afflicts those relations.

"If the South would keep the Negro and have him satisfied," says Mr. W. T. B. Williams in his report to the Labor Department, "she must give more constructive thought than has been her custom to the Negro and his welfare."

Decent wages, schools—"miserable makeshifts," *The Jackson Daily News* called the rural schools for Negro children—high schools, of which now there are almost none for Negro boys and girls; abatement of "Jim Crow" legislation and restrictions; safety from mob violence and lynching; "protection against constant irritation, insult, and abuse for no reason other than that he is a black man"—these are among the prescriptions for more tolerable conditions in the Southern states. If it were not for the color of the victims, the nation would rise in anger and abhorrence and see to it that the conditions which now prevail were remedied. If it is found troublesome or even unprofitable to attempt a cure of such deep-seated malignancy as the ignorance and prejudice and self-seeking which controls the relations of the races in this country, it will in the long run be found more unprofitable and troublesome not to attempt a cure. The South's "color psychosis," as I have called the instability and excitability of the public mind with reference to race, affects its entire life. It affects the choice of men to represent the South in the councils of the nation and thereby affects national policy for internal and on foreign affairs.

"The experiment," said Nathaniel Southgate Shaler, "of combining in a democratic society, in somewhere near equal numbers, two such widely separated races as the Aryans and Negroes has never been essayed. . . . It may as well be confessed that a true democracy, social as well as political, is impossible in such conditions, and that any adjustment which may be effected must have many of the qualities of an oligarchy." [1]

There is no objection to the frank recognition of such a proposition as Doctor Shaler put forward and to acquiescence in it. But to proclaim democracy; to shout freedom and equality, and actually to maintain that pseudo-democracy by oppression and terrorism which compares favorably with the best efforts of the Turk in Armenia; to divorce the language of the politician and statesman so completely from the terms of the life he represents that every intelligent and enlightened man must smile at his pronouncements; to make integrity impossible because the South and the nation cannot face the deep division within itself—is to poison at their source the aspirations of the men whose faith looks forward to societies untainted by violence.

[1] *The Neighbor*, p. 180.

IV

ANTHROPOLOGY AND MYTH

"INEXORABLE doctrines on the inequality of human beings," says Jean Finot, "adorned with a scientific veneer, are multiplied to infinity. . . . Despotic, cruel, and full of confidence in their laws, the creators and partizans of all these doctrines do their best to impose them as dogmas of salvation and infallible guides for humanity."[1] The methods used to establish the inequalities of which M. Finot speaks are almost as various as the doctrines themselves. Some persons proceed from a dissected human brain and a set of scales to draw conclusions applicable to the politics of a fifth-rate village. Others, their senses sharpened to a degree which would make any dog envious, detect race by odor, as the hero of Shaw's *Pygmalion* could detect nativity by accent. Given an absence of

[1] Jean Finot, *Race Prejudice*, translated by Florence Wade-Evans, 1907. New York: E. P. Dutton Co.

irony and self-criticism in a community as orthodox as the Southern states, the most extreme statements find adherents. Assertions which, isolated from their context of assumptions and passions, would be sharply challenged become commonplace. In any attempt upon race relations, then, before it is useful to suggest plans and procedure, it is necessary to clear away the intellectual rubbish that prevents even formulation of the problems. Especially is this true of the relations of Negro and white in the United States; for in no civilized community in the world are more amazing assumptions current and confident affirmations made with less solid knowledge to which to refer them.

M. Finot himself speaks of the effect which the ideas of Gobineau exercised upon the philosophy of modern Germany. It was Gobineau, it will be recalled, who discovered that the best of civilization is due to the Germanic races, whose blood sustains modern society. He it was who as much as any one man popularized in Germany the notion of superior and inferior races. "It has been found," remarks M. Finot, in comment, "that Gobinism displayed too much pessimism in the face of too little knowledge, and that even its ideas of barbarous and inferior peoples lacked clearness." But the United States has its own Gobinism which takes over almost bodily his style of argumentation and the assertions made later, under the influence of Darwinism, by Lapouge. If universal history becomes "reduced to the history of the variations of cerebral structures," many Americans would extend the process from history to prophecy and predict the future on the basis of cranial measurements. In this connection there is more than passing interest in M. Finot's statement that for Gobineau "it is only a matter of bringing his contributions to the great struggle against equality and the emancipation of the proletariat." For the American Negro has been the proletarian *par excellence*, and the motives to keep him a proletarian have been strong.

It is the evangelist, animated by religious fervor and race patriotism, that presents the extreme of opinion on race matters in this country. He is as devoted to racial purities and ascendancies as was ever an apologist of Teutonic hegemony. The evangelist's statements, unlike the propositions hazarded by scientists, have the advantage of being true for all time. No apology is necessary, therefore, for offering in evidence the remarkable information with which an American regaled the world so long ago as 1905 in *The Color Line*, whose subtitle reads, "A Brief in Behalf of the Unborn." The author, William Benjamin Smith, wrote from Tulane University. It is safe to say that the beliefs and opinions he voiced at a time when the South was smarting under the sting of the invitation to dine extended by President Roosevelt to Booker T. Washington still pass current.

What is the main issue for Mr. Smith? How does he attack the manifold questions of judicial procedure, office-holding, trade-unionism, municipal politics, housing? His answer is simple: The South "stands for *blood*, for the '*continuous germ-plasma' of the Caucasian race.*" That Northerners and Europeans may choose their associates and such table company as they please is conceded. But "in the South the color line must be drawn firmly, unflinchingly—without deviation or interruption of any kind whatever." There is a *tu quoque* for the Northern capitalists, who could hardly maintain that their "ruling corporate powers" are even barely just "toward the poor and humble, in the administration of the important industrial trusts which God has so wisely placed in their hands. They are giants, and it is in the nature of giants to press hard."

Comparatively, then, the South is sinless. On the merits of her own case the South "is entirely right in keeping open at all times, at all hazards, and at all sacrifices an impassable social chasm between black and white. This she *must* do in behalf of her blood, her essence, of the stock of her Caucasian race." The alternative is mingling of the races. "It would make itself felt at first most strongly in the lower strata of the white population; but it would soon invade the middle and menace insidiously the very uppermost. . . . *As a race, the Southern Caucasian would be irreversibly doomed.*" Mr. Smith is so quotable that restraint is necessary in appropriating his eloquence. "No other conceivable disaster," he says of race mixture, "that might befall the South could, for an instant, compare with such miscegenation within her borders. Flood and fire, fever and famine, and the sword—even ignorance, indolence, and carpet-baggery—she may endure and conquer while her blood remains pure; but once taint the wellspring of her life, and all is lost—even honor itself. It is this immediate jewel of her soul that the South watches with such a dragon eye, that she guards with more than vestal vigilance, with a circle of perpetual fire." As guardians of the South's vestal fire, one is tempted to offer Mr. Smith volunteers from the three million to five million mulattoes of the United States. "It may not be that she is conscious of the immeasurable interests at stake or of the real grounds of her roused antagonism," adds Mr. Smith, very truly; "but the instinct itself is none the less just and true and the natural bulwark of her life." Upon what is the justice of the South's instinct, as formulated by Mr. Smith, based? Simply upon the proof "craniologically and by six thousand years of planet-wide experimentation" that "the Negro is markedly inferior to the Caucasian," and that "the commingling of inferior with superior must lower the higher." Education and civilization are "weak and beggarly as over against the almightiness of heredity, the omniprepotence of the transmitted germplasma. Let this be amerced of its ancient rights, let it be shorn in some measure of its exceeding weight of ancestral glory, let it be soiled in its millennial purity and integrity, and nothing shall ever restore it; neither wealth, nor culture, nor science, nor art, nor morality, nor religion—not even Christianity itself. Here and there these may redeem some happy, spontaneous variation, some lucky freak of nature; but nothing more—they can never redeem the race. If this be not true, then history and biology are alike false; then Darwin and Spencer, Haeckel and Weismann, Mendel and Pearson, have lived and labored in vain." What has any controversialist to offer against Mr. Smith who would bet the world's history and science on the truth of his assertions, who asserts that a man "may sin against himself and others, and even against his God, but not against the germ-plasma of his kind"? For "if the best Negro in the land is the social equal of the best Caucasian, then it will be hard to prove that the lowest white is higher that the lowest black," and Darwin will have lived in vain. Lest it be thought that few will follow Mr. Smith, who, like Ibsen's Brand, seeks "*alles oder nichts*" among the inaccessible pinnacles of absolutism, he assures the reader that he has "some acquaintance with some of the best elements of the Southern society, some of the best representatives in nearly all the walks of Southern life"; and those elements will never waver a hair's-breadth from "uncompromising hostility to any and every form of social equality between the races."

Mr. Smith's doctrine, then, is resolved into an affirmation, for which he offers proofs, that the Negro is "inferior" biologically to such an extent that no education or civilization could bring him up to white men's standards; that racial mixture would result in disastrous "mongrelization" of the "Caucasian race," and that an inevitable corollary of the abatement of rigid barriers against "social equality" of the Negro and members of the "Caucasian race" is this mongrelization. Therefore, let the Negro remain on the plantation and in "personal and occasional service . . . where his abilities may be most naturally and most profitably employed." The Negro, like other "backward peoples," has "neither part nor parcel in the future history of man." Race transcends individual considerations. "There is a personal and even a social morality that may easily become racially immoral." In the interests, therefore, of the purity of Caucasian germ-plasma, the Negro is to be denied the, for him, useless higher education, is to be used as a plantation laborer or servant, and to be allowed, at the convenience of nature, to become extinct. Even membership in labor unions will never be accorded the "negroid," and the plans of Booker Washington and "his Northern multimillionaire admirers" for making skilled laborers of the Negro cannot succeed in solving the race problem.

Another Southerner, of a different stamp, who has accepted the postulate of modern anthropology that all races of men are kin, and therefore hesitates to ally himself with Mr. Smith and the angels, contributes first-hand description of the Negro pertinent to this discussion. The Negro, Mr. W. D. Weatherford[1] finds, is lacking in self-control. "To him the future has little meaning." This lack is explained by the exigencies of the tropical climate under whose influence the race had dwelt. Likewise the native of the tropics is led into a form of sexual indulgence "which seems nothing less than terrible." "The next weakness of Negro character which stands out prominently is superstition." Fear of angry spirits, "of the power of the fetish," have to a degree "become so deeply ingrained in the nature

[1] *Opus cit.*

of the Negro that the slaves and their descendants have never been able to shake themselves free from its terrible hold." Hence the Negro's conservatism. Cruelty to animals and dependents is another character which Mr. Weatherford lists: "Some of the horrible practices of punishment in Africa would be unbelievable did not one have the thought of the Inquisition, St. Bartholomew, the French Revolution, ever staring him in the face." The portrait of the Negro is then still further elaborated with vanity and conceit, wordiness, and absence of the power of initiative. As against these shadows, Mr. Weatherford opposes the Negro's fidelity. "In fact," he remarks, "if I must deal with a shiftless man, I believe I would take my chances on a trifling Negro rather than a trifling white man. Not a few of the managers and owners of large plantations have expressed to me this same preference." That fidelity which was supposed to be characteristic of the old-time Negro survives in the "new Negro." "They may lie or steal in petty ways," says Mr. Weatherford, "but even the poorest type of Negro rarely betrays a specific trust." Add to these traits gratitude, generosity, the absence of malice or a revengeful spirit, kindliness, a sense of humor, religious sense, love of music, "souls responsive to the truest of musical rhythm." "What if the race is not the most brilliantly intellectual? What if they are lacking in self-mastery? What if there is often a lack of industry and thrift?—here is a catalogue of race traits enough to make any race happy, virtuous, useful, and even great." Thus two Southerners.

It will perhaps be advantageous to list the characteristics of the Negro as they are given by Messrs. Smith and Weatherford, and to add to them such as will be recognized as passing current. The list might read somewhat as follows:

Against

1. "Inferior" biologically as indicated by abnormal length of arm, prognathism, brain weight and structure, eye coloration, flat nose, protruding lips, large zygmotic arches, size of face, thick cranium, weak lower limbs, skin color, "woolly" hair, thick epidermis, "rancid" skin odor, cranial sutures.
2. "Inferior" culturally.

For

1. Faithful.
2. Kindly.
3. Generous.
4. Musical (rhythmically).
5. Grateful.
6. Religious.
7. Lacking in malice and vengefulness.
8. Physically stronger than white.
9. More resistant to certain diseases and even immune to some.

Against	*For*
3. Intellectual development stops at puberty.	10. Adaptable to climate and culture.
4. Immoral (sexually).	11. Persistent, racially.
5. Uncontrolled as to appetites and subject to "primal emotions" such as fear, anger, jealousy, self-exaltation, self-depreciation, sorrow.	
6. Superstitious.	
7. Cruel.	
8. Conceited and wordy.	
9. Shiftless and lazy.	
10. Lacking in initiative.	
11. Deficient in reasoning power and the "higher" intellectual processes.	
12. Criminal.	

There are in addition certain qualities commonly ascribed to the person of color possessing some admixture of white blood. Thus:

Against	*For*
1. "Degenerate" and "inferior hybrids."	1. Abler than the Negro of pure blood.
2. Physically inferior, succumbs easily to disease: lung capacity inferior, respiration rate unfavorable, never passes sixty years, "cachetic."	2. More intelligent than the Negro.
3. Listless.	3. Sturdier physically than the Negro.
4. Criminal.	4. Furnishes leaders of the race.
5. Short-lived.	
6. Fails to propagate.	
7. "Scrofulous, consumptive."	

It will be noticed that many of the characters attributed to Negroes and to colored men with white ancestry are contradictory. The whole field of science, from biology and chemistry to anthropology and archeology, is involved in the discussion, to which the explorer, the historian, the psychologist, the violently partizan amateur contribute their beclouding pronouncements. The tendency among men of science is to narrow the discussion from such all-inclusive terms as "racial inferiority" to measurement of specific aptitudes and characters. The characters of race and culture are so many and so complex that it is assuming omniscience to pretend to sum up all available knowledge, and, having weighed and balanced, to give final judgment for or against a race. Modern anthropology takes the position, with respect to the Negro, as with other races, that no direct connection between physical characters and abilities or aptitudes has yet been established. Thus even the possession of large or small brains does not postulate genius or stupidity. The measurement of ability by intelligence tests is still in its infancy, a development of, at most, the last twenty years. Nearly if not all of the scientific experiment such as the measurement of intelligence of school-children, of Negro and white races, is subject to criticism of method, in that it has not been possible to isolate racial characters from influence of social environment.

In an account of one experimental study of white and colored children of Richmond and Newport News, Virginia, the author, George Oscar Furguson,[1] ably summarizes the conflicting views entertained by scientists the world over. "One would not be far wrong," he remarks, "in saying that all of the experimental work done on the psychology of the Negro prior to 1900 is of practically negative value." And yet, on the basis of observations, often partial, more often uncritical and inaccurate, even scientists have dogmatized. Le Bon divided the races of man into four classes, of which the "superior," as contrasted with "primitive," "inferior," and "average," consisted in the "Indo-Europeans." G. Stanley Hall has repeated the assertion that the Negro's development is partially arrested at puberty. Bean, in his studies at Baltimore, came to the conclusion

[1] The Psychology of the Negro: An Experimental Study, *Archives of Psychology*, April, 1916.

that not only the anterior association center of the Negro's brain, but the whole frontal lobe, was smaller than the white man's, whereas Mall three years later concluded that "with the present crude methods the statement that the Negro brain approaches the fetal or simian brain more than does the white is entirely unwarranted." Mall, according to Furguson, "reviews the previous work done in this field, and comes to the final conclusion that there is no valid evidence to show significant brain differences from the point of view of race, sex, or genius." From the point of view of the psychologist, Woodworth in 1910, reviewing the work of himself, Rivers, Bruner, Ranke, McDougall, and Myers, said of the status of race psychology: "One thing the psychologist can assert with no fear of error. Starting from the various mental processes which are recognized in his text-books, he can assert that each of these processes is within the capabilities of every group of mankind. . . . Statements to the contrary, denying to the savage powers of reasoning, or abstraction, or inhibition, or foresight, can be dismissed at once. If the savage differs in these respects from the civilized man, the difference is one of degree, and consistent with overlapping of savage and civilized individuals."

It is therefore hazardous, to say the least, in the present state of information about race and race characters, to assert that any race is inferior and "incapable" of any known state of culture. Furguson's tests led him to conclude that "the average performance of the colored population of this country in such intellectual work as that represented by the tests of higher capacity appears to be only about three-fourths as efficient as the performance of whites of the same amount of training," and he indicated his belief that the difference is probably wider than the tests show. On the other hand, his tests did not show "the relative ability of colored and white persons in the intelligent handling of concrete materials." But just what the tests do show is open to question.

"It is always difficult to state just what mental function is experimented upon by a given test," says Furguson. "The various traits so overlap and are so dependent upon one another in their action that no one trait can be completely isolated." Meanwhile, it can be said without fear of contradiction that there is no authentic corroboration for the following statements: (1) that the mulatto is less hardy than the "pure" Negro; (2) that any difference in brain structure between white and Negro has been indubitably established; (3) that the Negro's mental growth "comes to a comparative standstill at adolescence"; (4) that the "relative merits" of pure Negroes and mulattoes have been definitely made known. Although most of the writers who "have dealt with the problem of the relative mental ability of the white and the Negro take the view that the Negro is inferior," yet, says Furguson later, "it is probably true that there are more people who believe in racial mental equality than the reviews would indicate; equality is taken for granted, as in the greater part of our school system and in our political life. [?] . . . It may be said that the main conclusion one may draw from a study of the literature bearing upon the mental side of our race question is that we have taken a step toward its solution, but that the problem is still a problem."

Despite the doubts and the lacunæ which modern science must confess to in its data on race, popular discussion, never especially responsive to subtleties, always seizes on extreme statements and makes general principles of them of universal application. In this feast of generalities, contradiction, enthroned as a sort of piratical goddess, sits and smiles evilly on folly. Thus the Negro, branded as lazy and shiftless, was credited by Shaler[1] with an ability to toil, "such, indeed, as has never elsewhere appeared in a primitive people." This same scientist, who asserts that in the Negro "the state-building capacities are lacking," is flatly contradicted by the observations of anthropologists, summarized by Lowie to the effect that the Negroes of Africa "are conspicuous for their ability to form large and powerful political states. . . . If we contrast Negro culture on the average not with the highest products of Dutch, Danish, or Swiss culture," he continnes, "but with the status of the illiterate peasant communities in not a few regions of Europe, the difference will hardly be so great as to suggest any far-reaching hereditary causes."[2] Furthermore, Mr. Lowie suggests, the determination of racial potentialities by the psychologist does not solve the problems

[1] Nathaniel Southgate Shaler, *The Neighbor*. p. 156.

[2] Robert H. Lowie, *Culture and Ethnology*, 1917. New York: Douglas C. McMurtrie.

of culture: "Even if an ultimate investigation should definitely fix the cultural limits to which a given race is hereditarily subject, such information could not solve the far more specific problem why the same people a few hundred years earlier were a horde of barbarians and a few hundred years later formed a highly civilized community." When the investigator has carefully accumulated and collated more facts than are available at present, his conclusions may become useful for American society. Meanwhile it is the sort of argumentation that appears in Mr. Smith's book which, imperceptibly almost, influences discussion of the Negro and of race relations even in the North. One may smile at any one's presuming to know what relative positions God has ordained for Negro and white man. But given a conviction on the part of one-third or one-half of the white group of a nation that a colored group is inferior; bolster that conviction with constant reference in the press to colored people as criminals; treat the Negro in public discussion as an amalgam of joke and calamity—and no public will be disposed to analyze the social conditions which tend to make the Negro with whom they may come in contact what he is. Much of what might be called the pro-Negro side of race discussion has been in the nature of negative evidence. For example, it is trumpeted far and wide that the Negro is racially and by nature a criminal. Statistics of crime are adduced in proof. Then the social scientist investigates and discovers that a far larger per cent. of Negro mothers than white must leave their families during the daytime in order to earn money, thus contributing to juvenile delinquency. He discovers that in Southern courts Negroes are convicted on evidence on which any white man would go scot-free. He finds that Negro vice, of which there is so much talk, is much more closely involved with the "superior race" than the reports of the newspapers would indicate. "The cry in the Southern newspapers against Negro dives," remarks Professor Hart, "generally ignores the fact that many of them are carried on by white people, and others are partially supported by white custom." [1] As contrasted with the looseness and immorality commonly ascribed to the Negro, there are such observations as those of Junod [2] of the elaborate

[1] Albert Bushnell Hart, *The Southern South.*
[2] Henri A. Junod, *The Life of a South African Tribe.*

ceremonial and religious restrictions upon sexual indulgence which guide natives of Africa. But in the conditions of modern news service, misstatements always find their way to a larger public than do corrections, partly because they are more frequent and more emphatic, partly because they are considered to possess more "news value" and are therefore boldly displayed, partly because such misstatements reinforce popular preconceptions. To such an extent is public sentiment formed by obvious fabrications that even those men who would voice the Negro's grievances must bow to prejudice.

In November, 1919, for example, *The Arkansas Gazette* published a transcript of an address by the president of Hendrix College. The speaker, obviously animated by the disastrous riots which had occurred in Phillips County in October, 1919, spoke of the necessity for examining the causes of discontent among Negroes, of establishing understanding and co-operation between leaders of both races. But he felt obliged to "sweeten" his remarks to Southern white men by saying that "the Negro is a child race" and is "weak, docile, and is easily controlled." He conceded that the Negro "has much of humanity in him—is good-natured and quick to forget wrongs." The phrasing is the more significant in that it came from a man who realized the dangers created by the prevailing injustice to the Negro, and was eager to make his hearers realize those dangers also.

Even cultivated Americans are too frequently unaware of the incertitudes of the scientist on questions involving race. But they are fed with certitudes, from the Southern press, of the "we know the nigger" type. Mr. Lowie has shown "how many factors have to be weighed in arriving at a fair estimate of racial capabilities, factors which are naïvely ignored in most popular discussions of the subject. We can, farther, say positively that whatever differences may exist have been grossly exaggerated." The process of gross exaggeration is a norm of public discussion of race relations. The mere fact of the mention of race in connection with crime, the repetition in head-lines of such epithets as "Negro Fiend," "Negro Murderer," the tacit assumptions underlying which have made it possible to associate race with fortuitous criminal acts, are a measure of the extent to which the South's color psychosis is shared by and colors the thought of the nation. Crime, except in so far as it is analyzed into the conditions which have produced it, consists of a series of symptoms. To talk of any civilization in terms of the crimes committed by members of its society is to talk about a living organism in terms of the symptoms of its disease. From no other point of view is severer criticism of the American press possible than from that of a citizen who desires less embittered suspicion and more understanding of Negro and white man for one another. Before the era of the World War the impress of such conformity of public opinion as prevails in the South was foreign to the rest of the nation. But even if there is not, as there was in Washington, in Omaha, and in Chicago, before the riots there, a deliberate press campaign to debase the Negro, continual and casual reporting of Negro criminality will have the same effect.

Washington has long been a border on which Northern and Southern attitudes toward race have met and been pressed in conflict. Technically the Northern attitude has prevailed, even under Democratic administrations; attempts to enact street-car segregation and other Jim Crow ordinances for the District of Columbia failed. One such measure was introduced at the very time of the riots. During the riots the Southern attitude prevailed. White men did try to show the Negro "his place." The conflict between Northern and Southern points of view, repeatedly checked as Jim Crow bills applying to the District of Columbia were defeated, then went over to the newspapers. The statistics of the Washington chief of police had little weight against the reports of a crime wave and flaring head-lines announcing that another Negro brute had "attacked" a white woman. The condition of hysteria which the newspapers effected was, presumably, local to Washington. It was obvious a press campaign was under way. Anti-prohibitionists were triumphantly pointing to the "wave of crime" in support of their contentions. The commissioners of the District of Columbia and the chief of police were involved in charges of poor administration. To any reader of newspapers to whom printed paper is not apocalyptic, ulterior motive was written over the face of the "crime wave" in which the newspapers were bathed. A critical attitude might have been expected of news-distributing agencies and of correspondents of powerful newspapers—that is, on the part of any one who had had no experience with news distribution. But the most inflammable misstatements were absorbed whole and were sent broadcast throughout the country. What was by admission of a commissioner of the District of Columbia a series of attacks by white men upon Negroes was distorted by a *New York Times* head-line into "Negroes again riot in Washington, killing white men," by *The New York World* to "Three are killed as blacks renew riots in capital," and by *The New York Evening Telegram* to "United States cavalry unable to quell Negroes." The white mobs were beaten back by Negroes themselves. But white mobbism won its victory in the newspapers. To a Northern public, not consciously affected by the rigidity of Southern sentiment about race, there came, nevertheless, news reports of a sort which that Southern sentiment would have exacted. Similar conditions prevailed with regard to the riots in Arkansas, in Knoxville, in Omaha. At the Southern end of the telegraph wires which feed the country with its news are frequently men either attuned to conformity on race problems or forced into it in virtue of the necessity for continuing to live and to earn in a white Southern environment.

To what an extent the South's color psychosis afflicts the nation few Americans realize unless their attention is called to such an exceptional performance as that of *The Chicago Daily News* in directing Mr. Carl Sandburg to report on race relations there. His investigations of the effects of the migration, real-estate ventures, industrial and labor conditions, the reflex of each lynching on the North, crime and politics, which *The Daily News* made available in a series of articles [1] should have commended itself as a matter of journalistic procedure to every Chicago editor at least. "Publication of the articles had proceeded two weeks," says Mr. Sandburg, "and they were approaching the point where a program of constructive recommendations would have been proper, when the riots broke and as usual nearly everybody was more interested in the war than how it got loose." But it was not until the war "got loose" that most editors took an effective interest in race relations in Chicago, and

[1] Republished as *The Chicago Race Riots*, 1919. Harcourt, Brace, & Howe, New York.

then in a number of cases they did so only to pour oil on the flames. The condition Mr. Sandburg describes is a characteristic one. No one is more interested in war, apparently, than American newspaper editors, and no one is less interested than they in how it gets loose. The mixture of cynical indifference, ignorance, and falsity with which race relations are treated daily, extraneous circumstances like the crime of a degenerate are fastened to race and the connection riveted upon the public mind, is the most sweeping commentary possible on the American approach to what is often called the nation's tragedy.

For the purpose of furnishing Americans with accurate information on race and race relations, modern science might almost as well not exist. "Blind devotion to the dogma of the natural inferiority of the black race" has indeed, as Mr. George Elliot Howard says, "cost the white race dearly. . . . In fact, for nearly a hundred years the intellectual energy of the South has been absorbed in the defense or protection of its cherished race dogma."[1] The process of transferring

[1] "The Social Cost of Southern Race Prejudice," *American Journal of Sociology*, March, 1917.

this fruitless and uninformed conflict to the entire United States, goes relentlessly on. "That lust is a racial 'instinct' in the Negro," continues Mr. Howard, "uncontrollable and ineradicable—is the sinister lesson taught by the novels, the dramas, the essays, the newspapers, and the political demagogues that have shaped public opinion in the South. The most suggestive epithets are devised to kindle the passions of the mob." If the press is an effective means of creating hatred and distrust, the motion picture has been shown no less effective. Dominated by fear, with minds closed to one avenue at least, divided against itself, sterilized and made to that degree inflexible in thought, the white South is yet an integral part of the United States, tied to popular emotion by every means of communication and intercourse. It seems almost exaggeration to say that colored people know more about the facts of race and of race relations than do white Americans. Yet, in many instances that is true. For where the white press shirks responsibility for presenting the analyses and then the obvious facts which would make race inequities glaringly clear, the colored press, sometimes with bitterness, takes up the burden. A white American desirous of a critical insight into the society in which he flatters himself he lives could not do better than read carefully a number of race-conscious newspapers published for and by Negroes of the United States.

Upon science, then, upon the carefully ascertained information essential to any community's progress, the South's color psychosis lays obstructions and fetters. Such information, in the state of the Southern public mind and press, cannot penetrate the Southern states. On the other hand, current misinformation and dogma, carried in every vehicle for creating and forming public opinion, emanates from the South to the rest of the country. Misinformation is the product not necessarily of the absence of means to truth, but of a closed mind. Upon the nation's life the closed mind of the South in matters pertaining to race has had a poisonous effect. The distinction of North and South is neither made nor is it perpetuated north of Mason and Dixon's line. It has been made by the South in virtue of a *Kultur* which a thousand semi-literate Treitschkes have been permitted to affirm from their editorial chairs, basing their ascendancy and that of their kind upon malignant and ignorant denunciation of the black man; upon hostility to the life of the modern world—scientific investigation.

V

CERTAIN EFFECTS OF WAR

"AGITATION of the Negro question became bad form in the North," wrote Dr. Charles A. Beard, "except for quadrennial political purposes."[1] It is still bad form, despite the occasional resolutions offered in the Senate, to investigate over-representation of the South. The Negro, elevated to the vote and to political equality with whites, was dropped by the more "practical" Republicans after Reconstruction days, when the "cash nexus" of North with the South had been once more formed. Since the earliest days of American political life it has been bad form to agitate the Negro question. First, it pierced the glamour of religious and political idealism that was made to surround the nation's beginnings. The integrity of American Revolution itself was qualified. "In Jefferson's original draft of the great

[1] Charles A. Beard, *Contemporary American History*, p. 22.

Declaration there was a paragraph indicting the king for having kept open the African slave trade against colonial efforts to close it," says Phillips, "and for having violated thereby the 'most sacred rights of life and liberty of a distant people, who never offended him, captivating them into slavery in another hemisphere, or to incur miserable death in their transportation thither.' This passage, according to Jefferson's account, 'was struck out in compliance to South Carolina and Georgia, who had never attempted to restrain the importation of slaves and who on the contrary still wished to continue it. Our Northern brethren also I believe,' Jefferson continued, 'felt a little tender under these censures, for though their people have very few slaves themselves, yet they have been pretty considerable carriers of them to others.'"[1] Before ever the Negro himself began to look about the American political scene and to criticize principles and professions the spirit was abroad among white Americans. But for the most part the anomaly was resolved by intensity rather of idealism than of criticism.

The more vehemently Americanism, free-

[1] Ulrich Bonnell Phillips, *opus cit.*, p. 116.

dom, and equality are affirmed publicly the less pressing does it seem to examine just what they practically and individually imply. There is room for a study of American idealism as it is rooted in race relations. If the Republican party has been dominated at various times by practical men who preferred a mixture of ethical principles and industrial *laissez-faire*, the Democratic party has been utterly tethered. Democrats might rejoice in Andrew Jacksonism, but liberalism in a modern sense was denied them; they could only chafe at the division with which even Woodrow Wilson's reliance on the North for sentiment and on the South for votes menaced their party. The Civil War, which is commonly believed to have established the freedom of the American Negro, was, in this sense, merely another symbol of the struggle and division which was endemic before 1861, and still continues.

It might be said that in the Civil War the armies of Lee had finally surrendered to Grant, but that the eventual victory had rested with the Confederacy, whose cast of mind, whose over-representation in the House of Representatives, have been almost unchallenged in the nation. "Under the original Constitution of the United States," says Doctor Beard, "only three-fifths of the slaves were counted in apportioning representatives among the states; under the Fourteenth Amendment all the Negroes were counted, thus enlarging the representation of the Southern states." The Fifteenth Amendment to the Constitution represented one of the idealist gestures which, at the time of the Declaration of Independence, Americans hesitated to make.

With the American Negro free, a voter, and seemingly given a fair field of opportunity, race relations enjoyed a period of disregard. You cannot really confer freedom upon people who do not demand and make their own freedom, it was assumed, and the "real Negro question" was said to be:

"Can the race demonstrate that capacity for sustained economic activity and permanent organization which has lifted the white masses from serfdom?" This is to make the "race question" again too preponderantly one of racial aptitude. Only by eventual alliance of the Negro with white labor, if that should come about, will the inadequacy of the statement be demonstrated.

Participation of the United States in the World War changed the symbol. But the thing symbolized, the struggle within the nation, remained. It was an external enemy which the American armies went out to contend with. But the essential struggle of the war will be found to have been within the United States. The struggle consisted again in an effort to make American idealism ring true. Often to the Negro, the focus of this struggle, the American point of view was cynically represented. One group of Negro soldiers were frankly and brutally informed that they were going to fight for democracy *in Europe*. For every group who met the fact in a frank statement, dozens found reason to come to that conclusion. What the World War seems again to have emphasized and crystallized is the futility of applying the phrases of political idealism to a set of problems which, like those allied with race relations, demand varied and resourceful manipulation. The conflict over race relations is not set at rest by the unquestioned prosperity and opportunity which the World War brought to many colored Americans. In a sense, that opportunity has only intensified the struggle. Probably, since the United States entered the war, more Americans could be found who are apprehensive of the future of race relations than there were before. Many colored citizens were satisfied with half-Americanism until hundred-per-cent. Americanism was blared and dinned into their ears. Under the circumstances it was expecting too much to believe they would cultivate deafness. Of the prosperity of families brought North and of the education of desire which comes with means to gratify wants, much may be ascribed to the war. But on the other hand, many Negroes say that their condition is, if anything, worse since the war. And progress which depends upon a shortage of labor and war wages is subject to fluctuation. Under the suggestive title, "Why Southern Negroes Don't Go South," Mr. T. Arnold Hill [1] of the Chicago Urban League summarized certain of the World War's effects upon Negroes. Queries sent to hundreds of Negroes living in the South elicited replies of this nature: "I fail to see any improvement"; "There has been no change for the better"; "Why, conditions are worse than ever."

One man wrote to *The Chicago Defender* saying: "After twenty years of seeing my people lynched for any offense from spitting

[1] *The Survey*, November 29, 1919.

on the sidewalk to stealing a mule, I made up my mind that I would turn the prow of my ship toward the part of the country where the people at least made a pretense at being civilized. You may say for me, through your paper, that when a man's home is sacred; when he can protect the virtue of his wife and daughter against the brutal lust of his alleged superiors; when he can sleep at night without the fear of being visited by the Ku-Klux Klan because of refusal to take off his hat while passing an overseer—then I will be willing to return to Mississippi."

Both in the North and in the South each increase in prosperity of the Negro made feeling about race relations correspondingly tense. In the South, as always, the tensity manifested itself politically. Putting the Negro into the army was fiercely resented because it made the colored soldier an "equal" of the white. The bitterness had its reflex in rural districts, where white determination stiffened that that equality should not extend beyond the army. One consequence of this tension was a recrudescence of the Ku-Klux Klan, with aggressive announcements in the newspapers calling upon white men, in the familiar language of the night riders of old, to gather for the defense of womanhood and the Southland. But colored Americans were being taught that fighting was not a racial prerogative, even if voting was. Their instruction was interrupted at times by a propaganda asserting that colored troops had failed and that France had requested their return to the United States because of sexual crimes. But the Secretary of War disposed of the propaganda by a vigorous statement proving its falsity; and Brigadier-General Sherburne on numerous occasions publicly praised the courage, the endurance, and the soldierly qualities the colored troops in his command had displayed under the most difficult circumstances. The propaganda, therefore, which became accepted gossip among many white men of the United States army, did not affect the Negro's sense of his own fitness except to intensify his feeling of the injustice of the treatment given him. A significant item of his education in international affairs was the cordiality of French people and its effect among white people in his own land. Of the disabilities that were imposed upon the Negro in the army the list is a long and cruel one. How color prejudice worked against the success of the nation's arms was indicated by Major J. E. Spingarn of the American Expeditionary Forces, who publicly accused Southern officers with treason, in that they preferred white ascendancy in the army to the measures necessary for efficiency and for victory. In a number of Southern states the quota of colored men drafted exceeded the white. Thus from Mississippi 24,066 colored men, as against 21,182 white, joined the colors; in South Carolina 25,789 colored men, as against 19,909 white; in Florida 12,904 colored and 12,769 white; and in Alabama, Georgia, and Louisiana the quotas of colored and white men were very nearly equal. Despite the objections which the white South made to the enlistment and conscription of colored men, every means was used to exempt as few as possible from military service. In many sections, says a former special assistant to the Secretary of War, the Negro "contributed many more than his quota; and, in defiance of both the spirit and letter of the draft law, Negro married men with large families to support were impressed into military service regardless of their protests and appeals, and their wives, children, and dependents suffered uncalled-for hardships. Local draft boards, in almost every instance composed exclusively of white men, were in a position, if so inclined, to show favoritism to men of their own race; the official figures of the draft reveal the fact that in many sections of the country exemptions were granted white men who were single with practically no dependents, while Negroes were conscripted into service regardless of their urgent need in agriculture or the essential industries, and without considering their family relations or obligations." [1]

The effect of excluding colored men from draft boards was made sufficiently clear in the first report of the Provost-Marshal-General, which showed that of every 100 colored citizens called, 36 were certified for service, and of every 100 white men called, only 25 were certified. Furthermore, of the registrants placed in Class I of the draft, colored men contributed 51.65 per cent. of their registrants as against 32.53 per cent. of the white. The Negro, Mr. Scott continues, "had practically no representation upon the draft boards which passed upon his appeals—an arrangement which was wholly at variance with the theory of American institutions."

[1] Emmett J. Scott, *The American Negro in the World War*, p. 428.

The record of the injustice and brutality of which the Negro was made a victim in the United States army is too long even for summary treatment. Commanded as colored soldiers were, for the most part, by white officers and non-commissioned officers, members of their own race being with few exceptions denied promotion, they were domineered over and insulted. Every sort of hardship was visited upon even the most capable of the comparatively few colored officers commissioned. The ranking colored officer of the United States army, who was subsequently sent as military attaché to Liberia, spoke of the unremitting efforts that were made to discredit and humiliate the black officer before the world and before his men. In every way possible colored soldiers and their officers in France were discriminated against. Thus, General Erwin, commanding the 92d Division, is reported to have issued "Order No. 40," that Negroes should not speak to Frenchwomen. "Carrying out this order," says Mr. Scott, "the military police overseas undertook to arrest Negroes found talking to Frenchwomen, while the white privates and officers were not molested. This led to a serious misunderstanding between the French and the Americans and to a number of brawls in which the white and black soldiers participated."

Propaganda by white Americans to discredit their colored brothers in arms even went to the length of a secret communication to French officers and civilians, issued from General Pershing's headquarters, warning them against treating "the Negro with familiarity and indulgence," the French public not having become aware of the "menace of degeneracy" which had created an impassable "gulf" in the United States between races. American opinion is represented as the being unanimous in regarding the black man "as an inferior being with whom relations of business or service only are possible." The Negro's vices, this astonishing document says, "are a constant menace to the American, who has to repress them sternly." Warning is given against "the rise of any pronounced degree of intimacy between French officers and black officers. . . . We must not eat with them, must not shake hands or seek to talk or meet with them outside of the requirements of military service."

Also, French people "must not commend too highly the black American troops, particularly in the presence of white Americans." "French officers and French civilians," says Mr. Scott, "as a rule, could not understand why the black soldiers should not be treated identically as white American soldiers; when French officers were alone with Negro officers the latter were treated with the utmost friendliness and consideration, and it was only when in the presence of American officers that they reluctantly observed the official order, inspired by race prejudice." Much matter has been published showing that white commanders made repeated and insistent requests that colored officers be removed. Colored soldiers had, like colored laborers in civil life, to do the hardest and most disagreeable work of the army. They were assigned to coaling and stevedore duty frequently under imputation of lack of courage or ability. One Negro officer, at the close of a letter setting forth the difficulties he had had to endure, remarked:

"I am beginning to wonder whether it will ever be possible for me to see an American white without wishing that he were in his Satanic Majesty's private domain. I must pray long and earnestly that hatred of my fellow-man be removed from my heart and that I can truthfully lay claim to being a Christian."

On the civilian Negro, as well as on the colored soldier, the requirements of war were frequently made to bear with exceptional rigor. A survey of compulsory work laws and their enforcement led the investigator to conclude that "many employers of Negro labor in the South utilized the national emergency to force Negroes into a condition which bordered virtually on peonage. . . . No one," he adds, "can tell how far the system extended, as most of the offenses occurred in the smaller towns and communities where Negroes dare not reveal the true conditions for fear of punishment, a fear which is well founded, as the lynching record of 1918 will testify." [1] It would be idle to pretend that disillusion and bitterness did not follow in the wake of the military and civilian discrimination against the Negro. For the most part it was expressed in migration of colored people from the South. Unquestionably it found vent in the violence and the riots that made melodrama of race relations during the war, but especially in 1919. Never before to such an extent had the Negro fought back to

[1] Walter F. White, *The New Republic*, March 1, 1919.

repel white mobs as in Washington and Chicago. Hounded in the South, denied protection, whether from labor unions or from city officers in the North, the Negro armed himself. A condition for which white Americans were primarily to blame was laid at the door of the Negro. The most fantastic stories emanated from Washington, especially from Representative Byrnes of South Carolina and other Southern members of the House, later from the Department of Justice.

The Lusk Investigating Committee of New York State made the alarming discovery that Socialists were actually trying to "convert" colored men to Socialism. Editorial comment of the less windy sort was represented by *The Springfield Republican*, which, adverting to the Lusk Committee's discovery of the plan to "convert" Negroes, remarked: "If there was anything unlawful in such a program—assuming of course that no violence was to be preached—we fail to see it. But the Lusk Committee 'expressed amazement,' and Senator Lusk said that he regarded this evidence of a detailed plan for the spreading of 'Bolshevist' propaganda among Negroes in the South as the greatest menace the evidence before the committee so far had disclosed. The grim irony of the situation is that the very first point in the plan was that 'all acts of injustice to the Negro' were to be condemned. Perhaps that is revolutionary! God save America if it is!"

"Reds Try to Stir Negroes to Revolt" announced *The New York Times* in July, 1919, and a few days later, "Radicals Inciting Negro to Violence." "Negroes of World Prey to Agitators," said a *Times* scarehead in August, and *The New York Tribune* announced a few days later a "Plot to Stir Race Antagonism in United States Charged to Soviets." Officers of the Department of Justice were quoted as saying that "charges of an organized propaganda made in the House yesterday by Representative Byrnes, Democrat, of South Carolina, seemed to be well founded. . . . Agents of the Department of Justice are investigating. Facts thus far developed lead officials to believe that I. W. W. and Soviet influences were at the bottom of the recent race riots in Washington and Chicago." "United States Reveals Sedition among Negro Masses," said the caption of an article widely distributed over the country under the signature of David Lawrence, and

"Radicalism among Negroes Growing, United States Record Shows," announced *The New York World* in November of 1919. Despite the hysterical newsmongering inspired by Southern representatives, to which the Department of Justice was made a party, no connection between Russian or any other Soviet and Negro citizens of the United States was ever publicly established. Not enough evidence was accumulated by the loquacious investigators of the Department of Justice and their garrulous chief to procure the indictment of a single Negro of importance in the United States. They did succeed, however, in spreading a poisonous mass of misinformation and distrust. So persistent was the campaign of calumny that a group of colored editors were finally moved to appeal to the Attorney General to lay open before the country the basis for his insinuations or else to cease his propaganda. A letter from them to the Attorney General, widely published in the Negro press, stated that in the nation-wide campaign against "Reds and I. W. W. agitators" not a single colored person of the United States had, to their knowledge, been arrested. Colored people, said the letter, would continue to demand every right of

American citizenship under the Constitution. "These things colored people are agitating in the right way and with the proper spirit. There is an exceedingly small percentage of radical colored newspapers among us, and for that reason the colored press as a whole should not be labeled as radical, and should not be classified with the Reds and I. W. W.'s." It will be remarked that the South's color psychosis became extended, during the war, throughout the nation, not in virtue of justifying fact, but chiefly through a press campaign initiated by a Southern member of the House of Representatives. The conservative press treated the Negro very much as an alien enemy. His grievances were ignored. Numerous articles were published to establish how well the Negro was treated in Mississippi, how prosperous colored people were in Louisiana, how the South wanted colored workers to return from the North. But the migration northward was continued at the very time these inspired stories were appearing in Northern newspapers.

Although intelligent white Americans did not take seriously the innuendoes published by the Attorney General and the Department of Justice, propaganda charging the

Negro with "sedition" and "radicalism" was undoubtedly contributory to violent feeling and to conflict. The result was a presumption against colored people in the United States most oppressive as always to the more prosperous and intelligent men and women. The report of the Department of Justice, which was transmitted to the Senate in November, 1919, included a number of pages devoted to Negro magazines and newspapers. Editorial utterances had become more acid and more incisive since the war. The Attorney General spoke of "sedition" and "radicalism," but he failed to prosecute. In fact, Negro editors were guilty, not of sedition, but of indignation at brutalities and wrongs which the nation unprotesting had permitted to go on. The Attorney General found, what every student of race relations might have told him he would find, "the increasingly emphasized feeling of a race consciousness" among colored people. That the Attorney General characterized this race feeling as "openly, defiantly assertive of its own equality" is a commentary on his state of mind rather than on the facts. Throughout the Negro press, as among orators and the masses of workmen and the bourgeoisie, realization had come that the "old Negro" was going never to return. Servility and submission to wrong had been proved experimentally to be poor policy. Those Negroes who followed the prescription which Booker Washington had offered—work and thrift as opposed to political and civil demands—found that their work and their merit, whether its measure was financial or social, availed them little. They found class discrimination increasing, and moderate and intelligent white men less than ever able, apparently, to check the lawlessness represented in lynching and intimidation of every sort. Colored men found that the "good nigger" who bowed to white ascendancy and took orders uncomplainingly was eventually despoiled. The Negro who stood his ground and cleaved to his rights with his manhood and a rifle to defend him often won the respect if not the affection of his white neighbors. "Shoot Back to Stop Riots" is *The Boston Herald's* caption summarizing advice given to colored people by one of their leaders in November of 1919. It is the sort of advice with which they had been becoming increasingly familiar and had found in practice most effective.

When the division brought about by the

war became sharp, the occasional friend of the Negro, the Republican party, again began to withdraw. The Negro confronted the Democratic party which, no matter what liberal impulses it might derive from the North, would never help him in the South. The Southern Republican party was, as always, rent into two factions of which one was composed of "lily-white" Republicans who sought to curry favor with the white South by repudiating the Negro, and a lean faction which, in order to obtain offices under Republican National administrations, sought to maintain its influence over the colored voter. Politically, therefore, the Negro was without real friends. The period of the World War and 1919 especially, perhaps, became an era of change for colored Americans, who then came to realize as never before that only by themselves organizing, by defending themselves personally, politically, and industrially, could their position in the United States be made tolerable. Colored workers, it will be shown in a later chapter, acted independently of white labor organizations and were mostly victims, partly players, in the contest between capital and labor. The character of riots changed in

1919. They were not massacres of colored people. White men died. In a number of cities in which riots had been planned, notably in Memphis, Tennessee, and in Montgomery, Alabama, they did not occur because it was generally known that colored men were armed and were prepared to defend themselves.

The change, for the most part industrial, which the war effected in the South was in many respects a revolution. It was hardly more difficult for the South to face political emancipation of the Negro than to contemplate his industrial emancipation. Both were brought in view by war industry and war migration. That the war should at once make the Negro conscious of his prerogatives as a citizen, give him opportunity to earn the gratitude of the nation, make for him preferred opportunities as a skilled workman, and enable him to leave the agricultural communities in which he was most consciencelessly exploited, was bitter.

"One of the most serious of the long-standing grievances of the Negro," says the Labor Department's report on the migration of 1916–17, "is the small pay he receives for his work in the South."

The South's first response to the migration

included attempts to stop it by heavily fining and imprisoning labor agents, by intimidation of Negro migrants at railway stations, forcing many a colored farm tenant to flee by night in order to come North. Gradually it was realized that the competition of Northern industry, with its comparatively lavish wages, would have to be met. It also came to be understood that Negroes would go where their children might have the advantages of schooling. It was found that the migration was least from the districts in which there was no lynching and mobbism, where Negroes were permitted to enjoy the products of their labor in peace. The elaborate propaganda, directed chiefly at Negro migrants in Chicago, describing the prosperity and contentment of colored people in Louisiana, Texas, and Mississippi, was a measure of this understanding. As Mr. Hill has shown, all too frequently the news stories represented a desirable rather than an actual state of affairs. But a general realization by white men that the Negro must be satisfied in order to keep him on the land, that elements in that satisfaction are education for his children, human and decent treatment, and eventually even that most taboo instrument, the vote, is a long step toward progress in the administration of race relations. The war, which first gave the South opportunities to exploit Negro labor by enactment and enforcement of "work or fight" laws, provided the Negro with opportunity for bringing his exploiters to their senses.

If the war made the white South more than ever determined to show the Negro "his place" when he came home from the war and from "Frenchwomen," it made the Negro more politically self-conscious than ever before in his history in this country. He came to look critically upon his erstwhile friends, the Republicans. He began to break the mold of his former undeviating allegiance in order to listen to Socialist, class-conscious propaganda. He found himself spoken of as a race, treated as a political entity within the United States, and consequently he began to feel the intensified race consciousness of which the Attorney General made mention. The Negro citizen's weapon against discrimination of every sort was his economic value. His departure became a grave menace to the welfare and even the solvency of many portions of the rural South. His arrival in the North increased the hostility of trade-union members, but caused the union executives seriously to ponder the effect of excluding him. However he was treated, his strategic position was improved. That is not to be taken as a step in the harmonizing of race relations. Eventually it may mean that in the period of the war the problem of the living together in the same state of colored and white men was made immensely more urgent and more menacing. The Negro's political education, given an enormous impetus by his war experience, is being carried forward. Never before particularly concerned in the doctrine of class struggle, he is having it preached to him by his own newspapers and magazines which are quick to seize upon the economic motives of his detractors and exploiters. His own experience supplies many examples to supplement the arguments of his mentors.

Any colored person of intelligence necessarily began to analyze his condition in times as disturbed and as disturbing as those during and immediately following the war. To both white men and colored men the war demonstrated that the Negro has an economic place in this country if he is allowed to occupy it; that his departure in large numbers from the land in the South means loss in values and in productivity; that he is adaptable to industry in the North; that he must be considered as an element in the industrial struggle of capital and labor; and that in many a Northern city and state class-conscious or race-conscious appeals to groups of white men will be met with the ballot by large and increasingly well-organized groups of colored people, whose vigilant press keeps them informed of what affects their welfare. The foregoing summary, like all summaries, is over-simplified. It will be shown in subsequent chapters that in many localities the Negro is still treated with greater disregard and brutality than in slavery days; that his oppression cries to all Americans for denunciation and redress. But the way of hatred cannot stop the new emancipation which the war enormously accelerated. At most and at worst a policy of repression, misinformation, and exploitation can bring about irreconcilable conflict and tragedy for colored and white citizens who might otherwise become immensely useful to one another. The old anomalies persist. The United States is still in the position internationally of a kettle when it comes to calling pots black. The

South still openly, boastingly even, disfranchises colored citizens. And democracy is made in the eyes of the discerning to seem far more tentative in the face of race problems than its loudest protagonists would have it thought.

VI

THE SCAPEGOAT OF CITY POLITICS

IT is in the cities that race relations are most poisoned by rumor and myth. No group in the nation has paid a heavier toll to corrupt municipal politics than the Negro. He has paid it not only in bad housing, inferior schools, poor lighting, paving, and policing. He has, besides, been used as a tool in elections and as a lightning-rod to carry off angers for which he was not in the remotest degree responsible. During the period of acute change that accompanied and followed the migration northward, the use of the Negro politically and deliberate attempts to foment race riots of magnitude were established beyond doubt. Many elements contributed to the disorders in Washington, in Chicago, in Omaha, and in Knoxville. To say they were due to any one cause would be to over-simplify. But that a major part was played by motives and contests outside the control of colored people is incontestable.

In three of the four cities the riots were preceded by a press campaign in which Negro criminality stared every newspaper reader in the eye, in the form of glaring head-lines announcing cases of assault and robbery. This was true of Washington, Chicago, and Omaha. In two of those cities, Washington and Omaha, bodies of colored people met and sent appeals to the newspapers to desist from their dangerous and inflammatory campaign. Omaha's riot, in the course of which a colored man was without trial shot, hanged, and publicly roasted in a city street, the mayor hanged until he was nearly dead, the court-house gutted and burned and irreplaceable records destroyed, occurred on September 28, 1919. On the 12th of April, six hundred members of the Omaha branch of the National Association for the Advancement of Colored People had met at the Zion Baptist Church to protest careless remarks of the Omaha chief of police and the press campaign. The meeting deplored "published cases of criminal acts alleged to have been committed by colored men," called attention to the emphasis which was put on the race of offenders, and urged "that the public press be called upon and requested to avoid creating a sentiment against the race by using in glaring and sensational head-lines expressions of special reference to the race." The resolutions were sent to the chief of police of Omaha and to the principal newspapers. A similar appeal was sent to newspaper editors in Washington, District of Columbia. In September the campaign which the press of Omaha had carried on despite all warnings bore fruit.

"Jail Burns in Omaha as Riot Rages—City in Tumult, Police Helpless as Result of Attempt to Lynch Negro Who Attacked Girl—Mob Slashes Hose; Prisoners in Peril—One Man Killed and Two Wounded—Colored Men on Streets Are Beaten."

The captions on news stories sent broadcast over the nation told the story of what had happencd on September 28th. "Race Riots in Washington Serious—Blacks Chased by Mobs Past White House—More Than One Hundred Badly Injured—Ambulances Busy All Night—Police Unequal to Situation—Marshall and Members of Congress Urge Use of Army to Restore Order." This was the story which the captions had told of the

National Capital on July 20th and 21st. With minor variants, the stories were similar: a record of mobbism in the streets of American cities, houses burned, citizens done to death, the police helpless and troops enforcing order at the point of the bayonet. What the news stories did not tell, and never told, was what had occurred in the months and years preceding to bring such conditions to pass. Reference was invariably made at the time of riots to the "increase in crime," to "attacks upon women, murders, holdups, and robberies" as being the cause of the disorder. Yet the records of the chief of police in Washington failed to show the "many assaults upon women" that the newspapers had been using to create a condition of hysteria. His statistics showed four assaults upon women in the District of Columbia in June and July, of which three were attributed to a suspect under arrest at the time of the riots.

A typical example of the manner in which the Negro was victimized by the press of Washington occurred on August 15th, at a time when the memory of the July riots should have suggested caution. On its front page *The Washington Post* carried the caption: "Attacked by Negroes—Mrs. Minnie Franklin Injured at League Park Carnival—Two Assailants Get Away." There followed accounts of headquarters detectives searching for "two young Negroes" who had "covered" the woman with a pistol during the attack. On the following day, inconspicuously, on an inside page, *The Washington Post* retracted its glaring assertions of the day before with: "Calls Assault a 'Story'—Mrs. Franklin's Charge Against Two Negroes Dropped by Police." And it was developed that her narrative of the attack was a "fabrication." But the effect of the glaring scarehead of the day before could not be nullified and no attempt was made by *The Washington Post* to nullify it.

Of the Omaha press campaign before the disorders, a report by the National Association for the Advancement of Colored People said: "Every few days the papers head-line, 'Negro Has Assaulted a White Woman.' When investigated no truth is found in these statements. But raids follow and it keeps the branch busy seeing that the Negroes picked up in these raids are not treated unjustly. We have one case in particular in which we won a decided victory. A sixteen-year-old white girl claimed to have been assaulted by a Negro. For many weeks she refused to identify any of the Negroes brought before her. One day she saw on the street a man who fully answered the description of her assailant. She called the officer and had him arrested. Our committee happened to be in court on the day that he was brought in. The judge wanted to have his hearing right then without giving him a chance to prove his whereabouts on that date, but the lawyer insisted that he be given a chance. His trial was stayed one week. We sent telegrams to the men for whom he had worked and they answered as to his character; the foreman of the section gang with which he was working on the date of the alleged assault wired, proving an alibi, but the judge would not receive that as evidence. Then the foreman came, bringing with him his time-books, which had been sent to Chicago and O.K.'d. By this means we proved the man innocent because he had been over a hundred miles away from the scene of the crime at the time it was said to have been committed."

Another report describes the occurrences which were magnified by the newspapers into "Negro Assaults upon White Women": "In the case of a boy who was given ninety days," says the secretary of the Omaha branch of the association, "I was in court at the time of the trial. The little girl says the boy went past her and pulled her dress and she ran. The boy was seventeen years old. That was criminal assault.

"I have been at the trial of every case and the evidence is about as flimsy. One woman said that a Negro walked fast behind her. She called the police and he was charged with criminal assault. In the prison with the man who was lynched Sunday was a white man under bond for the same crime. If they were so eager to protect white womanhood they should have completed their work by taking him." These examples, which could be added to indefinitely, indicate the procedure. The Negro was to be tarred with the odium which is his in the South. "Rapist" was to be fastened as a distinguishing character to his color. Presumption so strong that it affected judges on the bench was created against accused Negroes. Not only was the Southern myth to take root in the North. It was so to affect race relations that colored people would be glad to return to the South whence they had come. Hence, after the Chicago riots the propaganda of improved conditions and prosperity in Louisiana and Mississippi. Hence the committees of white men to induce colored men to go South where they "belonged."

But it is the involvement of this propaganda in municipal politics that is to be shown. Nowhere was it clearer than in Omaha. As the presentation is one of fact, I make no apology for quoting at length and corroborating the report of a man long identified with "reform" of Omaha's city government. "There were many causes back of the riot in Omaha Sunday night, September 28th," he says. "For forty years Omaha was ruled by a political criminal gang that was perhaps the most lawless of any city of its size in the civilized world. There had grown up during that period a powerful group that lived on the proceeds of organized vice and crime." The writer enumerates three hundred and eighty-four houses of prostitution, saloons, and pool halls, and includes in the group "organized bank robbers, organized highway robbers, and professional 'con' men and burglars"—a list incredible to any one unfamiliar with the vagaries of American city government. This group decided in conference on the city officers to be elected, "and they would give the Boss for his service a certain sum of money and control of the vice interests, the police department, the police court, the juries, and then proceed to elect public officials." This condition prevailed without interruption until 1908. In that year an eight-o'clock-closing law was enacted for saloons and subsequently a jury-commissioner law and election-machinery law, taking both out of control of the "vice ring." State-wide prohibition was enacted in Nebraska in 1916. "In the spring of 1918, with the power of the vice ring thus weakened by the advances noted, the old political gang was almost destroyed. Thus we had eliminated the whisky interests . . . but we had not eliminated all of the gang. There was still left *The Omaha* ——,[1] which had been the mouthpiece of the vice ring. . . ." The remnants of former corrupt government combined "to destroy the present city administration and regain control of the police department. . . . In order to accomplish this, the paper, assisted at times by the two other daily papers, began a campaign of slander and vituperation against the police department of the city of Omaha, and in

[1] A newspaper.

order to make it effective they chose a line of propaganda to the effect that Negro men were attacking white women, assaulting them with intent to commit rape and actually committing rape, with the connivance of the police department. They made a majority of the people of Omaha believe that all Negro men were disposed to commit the crime of rape on white women." Attention of the mayor and the commissioner and chief of police was called to the association of lewd white women with colored men, and city officers were asked to get rid of both elements "for the safety of the colored people and the community." Police raids stimulated the press campaign against the administration, and the impression was created that the police were invading private residences without warrant and were arresting law-abiding citizens. The difficulties of the administration were intensified by remnants in the police department of adherents of the old vice ring, who "were doing everything within their power to hamper and discredit the honest efforts of the present city administration to enforce the law." The statement of Omaha's chief of police as to the composition of the mob, quoted in an earlier chapter, is borne out by this citizen, who says there was "in connection with the mob, fathered by these same influences, an organized gang determined to wreck the administration at any cost, and they deliberately organized a mob, furnished it with money and liquor, and the leaders of the old vice ring stood round in the mob urging the men to go in and assist in wrecking the court-house, lynch the Negro, and kill the mayor of the city, the commissioner of police, one of the police magistrates, and the morals squad, a group of detectives that had been relentless in enforcing the law against the criminal element." A police captain, the senior in the police department, who released fifty police officers on the afternoon of the riotous Sunday and sent them to their homes, is described as "a member of the old criminal gang" who had "served as a personal bodyguard, with another crooked police officer, to the 'boss' of the underworld." Some of the police officers were said to be in the mob encouraging attacks upon colored police officers who were endeavoring to maintain order. "The only reason the commissioner of police escaped was because, at the suggestion of the mayor and others, he was sufficiently disguised in his appearance to get out of the jail without being killed by the mob." The innocence is asserted of the Negro, William Brown, who was lynched, a contention which in view of his murder without trial can neither be established nor controverted.

"There have been published in the daily papers since May 1, 1919, thirty-six different cases of alleged attacks of colored men on white women," the informant continues, "and wherever there was any reference to an attack on a woman by any man the inference was always there that the man committing the assault was a Negro—that is to say, in no case was it ever stated where a white man had attacked a woman that the man making the attack was white." One such story was published in the inflamed state of the public mind immediately following the riot on October 1st. "Another Woman Is Victim of a Negro in Guarded Omaha," announced a scarehead of *The New York World* on October 2d. In the course of the news account occurs the following paragraph: "General Wood issued a statement at midnight in which he said Mrs. Wisner's account of the attack was incomplete and in part indefinite. 'There are some curious features to the case,' he said, 'Mrs. Wisner is unable to give any detailed account of what happened; *she is unable to say positively whether her assailant was a white man or a Negro,* although she seems to think that he was a Negro.'" In the prevailing hysteria it would not be difficult to "seem to think" any assailant a Negro. The elements leading to the Omaha riot are summarized by the informant as being three: "(1) an element that wanted to lynch a Negro because it was led to believe by propaganda that the Negroes were really committing these offenses against white women and were being inadequately punished for their offenses; (2) there was a political mob bent upon wreaking vengeance by the killing of the city officials, and (3) still another mob bent upon destroying all organized government and property, public and private."

The foreman of Omaha's grand jury, John W. Towle, substantiated in the main the statements of this citizen of Omaha. In submitting the jury's report he asserted that a primary cause of the riot was "a concerted effort on the part of certain citizens, officials, and part of the press to discredit the police force." "It is a well-known fact," said Mr. Towle's letter, "that there are two factions in the city and county political life. Those who believe in enforcement of law and order now have the control of the city commission and the police force. The leaders of the opposition have very frankly stated that they are in favor of certain kinds of vice, limited to restricted areas; that instead of licensing or suppressing same it should be openly tolerated. This system was in force during the past administrations and is capable of most extensive commercialism." Mr. Towle then asserted, as a matter of common knowledge, that "at least one party on Saturday night previous" to the riot went about to pool-rooms announcing that an attack would be made on the court-house "for the purpose of lynching this colored man." Such reports, he said, "were current about the city and were known in certain official circles, and just why this prisoner was not moved to the state penitentiary or some other suitable place for safe-keeping has never been satisfactorily explained, nor why these officials did not apprise Mayor Smith, Commissioner Ringer, and Chief Eberstein of their knowledge." Further corroboration came from the County

Attorney in Omaha, who, in a statement published by *The Omaha Evening World-Herald* of October 1st, lists in detail the "fake" stories used to discredit the police administration and to incite to riot. "One of the most popular of the fake stories that were used to incite the riot," he said in the course of his statement, "was that a colored man had attempted to assault a nine-year-old girl, was arrested, identified, and given ninety days in the county jail. The facts are that the little girl saw this Negro, and thought he was quickening his step toward her. She ran and told her mother. The Negro was arrested, but there was no evidence that he had even touched the girl or even run after her. . . . Still another story, positively false, was used in stirring up feeling that preceded the riot. It was said that a colored man was arrested for an assault upon a white woman, and that she identified him, but that he was later discharged. In this case her identification was very weak, and the prisoner established a positive alibi, bringing in from Iowa the white foreman of a road gang of the Illinois Central Railroad, who showed by his time-checks that the suspect was in Iowa on the day of the assault, and at work." The County Attorney draws a proper conclusion, "This sort of propaganda must cease, because it is false and incites to riot." The Governor of Nebraska made public acknowledgment of the dangerous propaganda when he remarked on September 30th that those "who have most to do with the molding of public opinion have constantly engaged in petty bickerings and criticism of the local officials which could not result in any but an utter disrespect of the law" (*New York Tribune*, October 1st). It was important for citizens of Omaha, said the Governor, to "organize their minds to discourage the activities of those who are constantly attempting to bring reproach upon public officials."

Industrial conflict formed, as is usually the case, an element in the Omaha municipal complex. The president of the Nebraska State Federation of Labor blamed the importation from the South of non-union Negroes for the disorder. "Crimes against women form the basis," he is quoted as saying (*New York World*, October 2d), "but the mob was given impetus by causes that are not apparent on the surface." Among these causes he enumerates the attempt by the "great employers of labor, including the packers," to "break down the wages of white labor" with imported Negro labor and the mayor's use of Negro labor "to fight the cause of capital against the just cause of the workingmen." "When the teamsters two months ago were on strike and were fighting for a living wage it was the mayor who put to work the ignorant Negroes of the South. He placed them on wagons. He used them as strike-breakers." Even this laborite has been "stuffed" with stories of assaults by Negroes upon white women. But he makes it quite clear that the white workman of Omaha does not want black men used to hold down wages. "If brought North they (the Negroes) must not be brought to fight the battles of capitalism. Every packer, every large employer knows what I mean by that." And of "the moment" when feeling in Omaha overflowed the shallow container called civilization, this laborite remarked: "Mayor Smith was regarded as an enemy. This feeling did not start the attempt to lynch him, but it helped to carry it along."

It will be seen that a detailed examination of the state of citizenship and city government in Omaha disintegrates "Negro Crime" as a cause of the riot of September, 1919. Properly, as *The New York Evening Post* remarked, the outburst could hardly be called a "race riot." Yet that was its characterization in newspaper scareheads throughout the nation. A casual or even an attentive reader of the news would have been forced to the conclusion that white men had been goaded to fury by repeated and unpunished attacks upon their women by colored men. Hidden and isolated paragraphs from various news accounts had to be gathered and assembled to give some picture of the moving forces which, according to the head of Nebraska's Federation of Labor, were not apparent on the surface. It is the surface only which the press scratches in its accounts of race relations. Where the press is used, as it was in Omaha, to be a tool in political contest, no analysis and exposition is to be expected for the people whom it is intended to bedazzle and to delude. The casual and adventitious reporter descending zestfully upon a scene of riot from otherwhere may absorb political gossip, and usually does. But he is expected to write about what happened, not about how or why it happened. His impressions are what people elsewhere in the nation, as well as the moralists and ethical guides who write editorials, are given to read. In the nature of existing news service, then, when part of the machinery of news distribution is the organ of political and moneyed factions and the rest of it is for the most part casual and superficial in its attack upon current events, the pictures created for the public of race relations and race disturbances must necessarily be grotesque caricatures.

Without duplicating or paralleling motives and events in Omaha, other centers of disturbance have presented situations obviously analogous. Mr. Carl Sandburg has made the political implications of the Chicago "race riots" tolerably perspicuous. He referred especially to a "city administration decisive in its refusal to draw the color line, and a mayor whose opponents failed to defeat him with the covert circulation of the epithet of 'nigger-lover.'" "The Black Belt of Chicago," said Mr. Sandburg, "is probably the strongest effective unit of political power, good or bad, in America." It was the Second Ward, formerly one of the best residence districts of the city, now including much of the Black Belt, that was credited with having elected Mayor William Hale Thompson in April of 1919. The Second Ward gave him more than 11,000 votes of the plurality of some 17,500 by which he was elected. Maintaining that Mayor Thompson was elected by the Negro vote of Chicago, an editorial, expressive of what many men were thinking, said of him: " . . . He lost much support, but made it up among those who cared nothing about such issues. Two white men practically control the Negro vote. These two men demanded concessions from the Thompson crowd in return for this solid vote. They received it in the shape of concessions to saloons, cabarets, dance-halls, and dives of various sorts. In the Black Belt all kinds of places were kept open till morning, while in other parts of the city they were required to close at 1 A.M." Testimony is uniform that the colored residence district was made to suffer from lax police administration, and that the exploitation of its voting power was in the hands of gambling-house keepers, white and black, and their patrons. "W. M. Bass has been operating craps and poker games night and day in the rear of a real-estate office on East Thirty-first Street," said Mr. Sandburg, "near Cottage Grove

Avenue. From an alley entrance at 3512 South State Street one may enter a temple of chance conducted by one McFallin. Two men known as 'Williams' and 'Kennedy' maintain a laboratory for the study of the laws of chance on South State Street, near Thirty-fifth Street, entrances front and rear. T. Jones has a similar laboratory on South State Street, near Thirty-ninth Street, second floor, front and rear entrances." Mr. Sandburg's account of the gambler's Mecca in the colored residence district hardly lacks circumstantiality. As for the victims of the gamblers, "who are naturally also the victims of the police who let the gamblers run the kind of games that are run: . . . Within two blocks were found a total of eighty-three families where 96 per cent. of the boys were truants from the public schools, and 72 per cent. of these boys were retarded at least one year by reason of truancy. In most cases the parents were away from home so much that they were out of touch with the children. . . . In thirty-one cases the father had 'deserted,' which means he is tired, dead, sick, or gone wrong from unknown causes. . . . In twenty-eight cases the father was a heavy drinker."

Where a mayor is elected by the vote of a

colored district; where the reward is given in the form of protection and immunity for those who profit from vice; where the mayor is known as a 'nigger-lover' in virtue of his administration's exploitation of colored voters—it is not difficult to demonstrate the connection of ill feeling between white and black men and politics. But it was not only by immunity to dive-keepers that the colored district was invidiously distinguished. In November of 1919, four months after the July riots, at the time when race antagonism was still vivid, accusations of discrimination were made in the distribution of funds for street cleaning. "Black Belt Favored in Cleaning Streets" read the caption of a Chicago newspaper. The news story reported that, although streets elsewhere were filthy, "the Black Belt ward, credited with re-electing Mayor Thompson, has not suffered in the care of its streets and alleys because of the financial stringency. . . . The Fourteenth Ward, which was carried by Mayor Thompson because of the heavy vote he obtained in the Westlake Street colored district, was not among those hit by the high cost of keeping the city clean."

Industrial or political as the causes of

disturbance may be shown to be, "race riots" is the careless descriptive term employed to designate it. A riot of more Southern complexion than that of Chicago occurred in Knoxville, Tennessee, in the last days of August, 1919. "Troops Fight Race Rioters in Knoxville," announced *The New York Times* of September 1, 1919; "Two Known Dead, More Than Score Injured After Two Days of Lawlessness—Army Lieutenant Killed—Accidentally Shot by Machine-gunners Who Were Firing on Attacking Negro Party—Mobs Loot Many Stores—Several Murderers Released in Attack on Jail, which Is Plundered of Money and Whisky." To judge by the caption a full-fledged race riot was in progress in Knoxville in which Negroes had formed themselves into "attacking parties." The uproar in which shops were looted, confiscated whisky stolen from the jail, "everything of value, including money, guns, whisky, clothing, and books," was taken, part of the jail records were destroyed, and white men convicted of murder were released from their cells and given liberty, was ascribed to one colored man who was referred to as the "cause of mob's riot." He was accused—but had not been tried—of killing a white woman by shooting. The "race riot" of Knoxville assumed a different complexion, however, when R. A. Mynatt, the local Attorney-General, was quoted in a despatch to *The New York Sun* of September 5th as being "satisfied that these men were bent on releasing white prisoners and looting, and camouflaged their work by pretending to want to lynch the Negro, Maurice Mays, then and now in jail at Chattanooga." The evidence obtained at the trial of white men arrested for looting and mobbism showed "that they did not visit the Negro floor, once they had gained entrance to the jail," and that "they set about at once to release prisoners and to plunder." An inconspicuous news despatch published in the *Sun* the following day, September 6th, bore the important information that "the old city [of Knoxville] was Democratic by a small majority, but the new city is Republican by from fifteen hundred to three thousand, depending on the way the women vote. Failure of the city and county officials in co-operating to prevent the recent outbreak between the races here has become a sharp issue in to-morrow's contests. A mayor will be elected and the eight highest of twenty candidates will engage in a run-off two weeks later to fill four places on the City Commission." The despatch is headed: "Knoxville Negroes Determine to Vote—Race Riots Laid to City Officers in Campaign Fight." The composition of the mob is indicated by the fact that of the first fifteen white prisoners to testify, only five had never been convicted or indicted before. The convictions against the others ranged "from one to more than a dozen," according to *The Knoxville Sentinel*, "and from small offenses to some of a more serious nature." Nevertheless, the Knoxville grand jury declined to indict the prisoners. Attorney-General Mynatt characterized proceedings as a miscarriage of justice and announced publicly that so long as he was connected with the criminal court none of the jurors would ever again serve on a jury. These facts, inconspicuous, or unpublished to the public, which had read in huge type of Tennessee troops fighting Negro race rioters, because a Negro criminal had murdered a white woman, hardly affected public information regarding conditions in Knoxville. Neither did the fact that Maurice Mays, the accused Negro, had been an active solicitor for votes in behalf of one of the candidates for mayor.

To *The New York Sun* of September 4th must be given credit for two further paragraphs illuminating the series of outrages. "Politicians, rival candidates for mayor in Saturday's election, are attempting," says one paragraph, "to capitalize the recent outrage to their advantage." "Members of the city police force," says the next paragraph but one, "passed out rifles and ammunition to members of the mob who broke into hardware-stores and pawn-shops."

Municipal politics did not, in Washington, play the same part as in Chicago, Omaha, and Knoxville. Appointive as is the Commission Government of the District of Columbia, there could be no such obvious intent to discredit the commissioners for electioneering purposes. However, the Washington police had been asking for increased pay and there had been agitation for new appointments to the force. In the House of Representatives, the mobbism in Washington's streets was at once turned to the account of the anti-prohibitionists, who asserted that prohibition encouraged just that sort of lawlessness. Washington's chief of police, furthermore, connected the obscene head-line display with which *The Washington Times* and *The Washington Post* greeted every new crime with the manifest desire of anti-prohibitionists to prove their contention that prohibition would be accompanied by a "crime wave." On the first page of *The Washington Post* of July 23d, a page lurid with lists of riot victims, tales of violence and brutality, one column had for its caption "'Dry Bill' Is Passed." The juxtaposition is the more significant in that to *The Washington Post* as much as to any one agency was due the hysterical fear and hatred which made the Washington excesses possible. Intoxicating liquor and race conflict occurred as twin considerations not only to *The Washington Post*, but to Representative Julius Kahn of California, a state favorably known for its grapes. On the occasion of his eighty-fifth birthday Cardinal Gibbons was interviewed by a representative of *The New York World.* On that solemn occasion the prelate took the occasion to say: "We are now afflicted with a war of races in the National Capital, where much blood has already been shed and lives sacrificed. Alas! it is a proof that a legislative suppression of intoxicating drinks is not, as it was said it would be, a panacea against all social and moral evils."

Washington has been adverted to as the meeting-ground of Southern and Northern attitudes on race matters. Southern sentiment looked hopefully to the outcome of the conflict in the capital's streets. Disgust was written not only on the faces of Southern Representatives, but in Southern newspapers, at the "leniency" with which colored people had been treated. It will be recalled that the riots had begun in a raid by white soldiers and sailors upon the colored residence district and the beating of unoffending colored men on the streets. Yet, said the Washington correspondent of a Memphis, Tennessee, newspaper on July 24th: "Southern Democrats here were sore to the core to-day. They were disgusted at the alien and 'uplift' radicals who prevented real action to clear up the situation." The "Southerners in the capital" were "disgusted beyond words with the actions of the District government, and the national administration, which acted almost entirely with a view of protecting the Negroes." The disgust was all-inclusive. "From Secretary of War Baker down to Chief of Police Pullman the entire conduct of the government during the riots was characterized by sissyism. The influence of aliens and of New England Negro elements prevented the vigorous policy which would have been pursued even in New York, to say nothing of Southern cities." The Southern remedy for conflict is then indicated: "The police failed to round up all Negroes and disarm them, as would have been done in any Southern city or almost any other place." The consequence of disarming the colored people of Washington, supposing that to have been possible, could hardly have been imagined, much less described. For, in the first two days of disorder, what kept white mobs from pillage, assault, incendiarism, and murder in the colored district of Washington was not police, but pistols and rifles in the hands of colored men.

Race tension in cities, it has been indicated, is definitely subject to manipulation by political leaders and their allies in newspaper offices. If that lesson was not learned in 1919, it will never be and the future of race relations in the United States is an ominous one. It is idle to talk about "solving the race problem" when cheap and mendacious newspapers, making claims to utmost respectability, are purchasable by political factions and deprive Americans of the one essential to democracy—accurate information on matters of public concern. The conditions in each of the cities whose riots have been examined does not differ essentially from that which prevails in the nation at large. The Negro's position is prejudiced by the Southern color psychosis whose victims proclaim their dogma with religious fervor. The Negro has been used as a bogy or a scapegoat, as the case may be, in the argument of every political and social question, from prohibition to the League of Nations. He has been stereotyped in the public mind as a criminal and a degenerate, and has therefore become a proper object of fear and hatred with which to play upon the imaginations of a misinformed electorate. It will be the work of years to undo the poisonous and anti-social accomplishments of such organs as *The Omaha Bee*, *The Washington Post* and *The Times*, *The Chicago Evening Post*, *The New York Times*, in fact, of the majority of American newspapers.

For the future, however, American public opinion can assure to itself certain minima of decency. It should be possible to prosecute newspapers which publish exaggerated and mendacious accounts of crime. It should be possible to discountenance the word "Negro" in bold head-lines when it is obvious the intention is to provoke hysteria that can find a vent only in mobbism and murderous brutality. It should be possible for white Americans to show Negro Americans in cities of the United States that they have some stake in city administration other than that which they now so often have to obtain through the political ingenuity of a few corrupt leaders. For the present, the only course for white Americans to pursue is to cultivate thoroughgoing skepticism as to everything which American newspapers publish about the Negro; and for colored Americans to insist, in so far as avenues of communication are not closed to them, on the facts being made known. Meanwhile, occurrences such as smudged the red, white, and blue of 100-per-cent. Americanism during 1919 suggest that there is work to be done in establishing government or at least peace in American cities.

VII

THE NEGRO IN INDUSTRY

Labor

THE World War helped to dispel the myth that the American Negro was at best an agricultural laborer only and that complicated industrial processes overtaxed his abilities. That myth was dispelled in the factories where colored workmen did white men's work and did as well as, and often better than, immigrants from Europe. In the course of the practical demonstration of their capacity as machinists and factory operatives, colored men not only established themselves in the North; their prosperity exerted a pull on their friends in the South, so that the migration, even after the signing of the armistice, alarmed Southern communities whose labor supply was being depleted. The immigration intensified many of the maladjustments of industrial society.

Congestion and overcrowding occurred in the cities to which the colored workers came. Bitter antagonisms were brought about between white labor unions and unorganized colored workers. Many white people, who had known color prejudice only in the offhand way of contempt, found their emotions feverishly active when their men and colored men competed for jobs or when, during a strike, places were filled with Negroes imported by hundreds from Alabama, Mississippi, or Georgia. The increased tension between the races to which the northward movement contributed had two main determinants. First, recognition by Northern industrialists that they must find some source of cheap labor to compensate the stoppage of immigration during the war, and that Southern Negroes were available for their purposes. Second, a realization by white labor-unionists that their unions were endangered by an influx of aliens, unorganized, distrustful of labor unions and therefore difficult and in many cases impossible, for the time, to unionize. What has been called "group protection" became a strong motive among white unionists. Independent as it was of racial antipathy—for hostility would have been directed against any laborers who threatened union standards—it speedily fastened on the color line. Thus, from the industrial movements and readjustments incident to the war grew new race conflict.

For the Negro, war-time opportunity was especially significant in that it enabled him, as he had never been able to do, to play with capital and with labor. In a short space of time Negroes found themselves preferred in many plants from which they had previously been excluded or where they had been employed in small numbers only. Their leaders urged them not to serve as strike-breakers, just as the more intelligent of the white union leaders had warned against dividing labor by the color line. In practice, white unionists had discriminated against the Negro, had given him no jobs when the allotments were made, or the most arduous and disagreeable work; had either discouraged his joining their unions or had made it virtually impossible for him to do so. In practice, the Negro, indoctrinated with the brotherhood of man and the common interests of all labor, irrespective of color, took advantage of the situation which presented itself. Colored workers in many instances saw no reason why, having always been made victims of white discrimination, they should fight the white unionists' battles.

The Negro's distrust of unionism, justified as it has been by discrimination in the North, is based on the treatment of colored labor in the South. It has been the rule to exclude Negroes from white unions. In June of 1919 it was reported that two thousand white unionists of Richmond, Virginia, had withdrawn from the Virginia Federation of Labor because W. C. Page, a Negro of Newport News, had been seated as a delegate. Under the circumstances, the American Federation of Labor at its spring meeting in 1919 indulged in a more or less empty gesture in voting, with but one dissenting voice, to admit Negroes to full membership. As is known, the Federation exercises little power over its constituent international unions. At the same convention at which the vote was taken, a representative of the Brotherhood of Railway Clerks justified the exclusion of Negroes from their union and announced that the color line would be drawn in the future as it had in the past. One of the colored delegates to the convention reported that in Virginia, from March to April, 1919, forty-three thousand Negro workmen had been obliged to join an independent labor union because they could not be received into those affiliated with the American Federation of Labor. The influence of Southern delegates to the Federation had always prevented effective measures to organize Negroes. Even where the constitution of the union contained no express prohibition, it was not uncommon for white membership to double while no Negroes were added, in an industry giving employment to both white and colored men. It is recounted in Epstein's *The Negro Migrant in Pittsburgh* that one labor leader reported a growth in membership of 100 per cent. in six months, in the Pittsburgh district. He said that there were no colored men in the union, although numbers had applied for membership and complaints had been made of discrimination.

"His statement concerning efforts to organize Negro laborers," the investigator comments, "would seem to have little meaning in view of his assertion that the growth of white membership during the past year was 100 per cent., while that of Negro membership was zero." This man's attitude is found typical of the "complacent trade-unionist." At the very time when it was claimed that the union was endeavoring to organize Negro workers, a white man who joined was reported to have been pledged as follows by the president of the union: "I pledge that I will not introduce for membership into this union any one but a sober, industrious WHITE person." Among labor leaders, too, are men born in the South, convinced that the Negro is inferior, and strongly adherent to the advantages of segregation and "Jim-Crowing." Through the influence of individual labor leaders and of delegates to the Federation, the Southern practice was made fairly general in the North while Negroes were not in a position to constitute a menace to unionism. With the demand for Negro labor to supply war-time and after-war needs, the scene changed. The Federation made its gesture of generosity. Unions whose strikers were being replaced suddenly discovered the brotherhood of man. The Negro found himself in a position of strategic importance. His skepticism regarding the advances of white unionists found expression in such news paragraphs as the following, from *The St. Louis Argus*, of July 18, 1919: "The recent Atlantic City meeting of the American Federation of Labor, at which the 'hand of fellowship' was offered the colored man, has not caused tradesmen of the race to jump pell-mell into the union band-wagon. In fact, it seems to have produced a reverse effect. The Negroes realize that they have become an important part of the working-class in industrial sections. The unions have, in the past, obstinately refused to admit them to membership or else placed them in auxiliary locals without direct representation. They cannot believe that this sudden change of heart is not backed by some ulterior motive." Every sort of opposition was offered the Negro during his progress to industrial bargaining power. Mr. Roger Baldwin, who worked as a manual laborer in the Middle West during October and November of 1919, writes:[1]

"Everywhere, of course, the Negroes had the hardest and most disagreeable jobs. Only the exceptional Negro had risen above the lowest paid day-labor rate. That's the rate I was getting, too! And it was these men I found really thinking, keenly conscious of the relation of their own problem to the race and to labor. Every one of the men

[1] Memorandum for which I am indebted to Mr. Baldwin.

was in favor of unions, but every one of them complained of union discrimination against the Negro. They are ready for organization which they feel would be fair to them.

"On the other hand, there was a feeling of desperation because of the almost universal ignoring or contempt of the Negro. Every man I spoke to talked of warfare between the races. All of them had arms or were going to get them. All of them were preparing to resist further invasion of what they regarded as their rights. They just didn't seem to have faith that white men, even in the unions, were going to make common cause with them. Even the scabs in the steel-mill at Homestead, Pennsylvania, where Negroes have been imported by the thousand, were all for the union and all for a strike at the right time, but they felt that they owed nothing to white men who had so long ignored and oppressed them. Not a single organizer had been sent into the Pittsburgh steel district. . . . I couldn't help but feel, as I looked around at the forces lined up about me, that the immediate future of American labor in many industrial centers depends on what the unions will do with the Negro.

It is the white man's job if he is to make the solidarity of labor a living fact." Mr. Baldwin found no "theoretical radicalism" among the Negroes. "I found," he says, "no trace of 'Red' propaganda, but I found observations and conclusions expressed in as 'Red' terms as I have ever heard them from a soap-box agitator. It is obvious that the conditions themselves produce radical thinking."

Discrimination against Negro labor bore fruit in the steel strike of 1919. The conditions which materially helped to engender the East St. Louis riots and the Chicago disorders were reproduced. Despite opposition in the South, where labor recruiters and agents risked death at the hands of a mob if their errand were made known, Negroes were brought North. Negro welfare workers were employed at the Homestead and Duquesne plants of the Carnegie Steel Company, at the Monessen plant of the Pittsburgh Steel Company, and by the Lockhart Iron and Steel Company. Three of the four basic mills of the United States Steel Corporation and the largest of the independent mills pursued the policy of encouraging employment of Negroes. During the first six weeks of the steel strike six thousand Negroes, it was estimated, were brought to Allegheny County. At Lackawanna before the strike there were said to be seven thousand employees, of whom seventy-two were Negroes. During the strike the mill was operated chiefly with Negro labor. Some of the steel-mills employed Negro preachers. Early in November a representative of the Urban League said that Negroes in the steel-works had remained at work during the strike almost to a man. There were, of course, exceptions, but in general, however favorably they were disposed to white labor unions, Negroes became effective instruments to be used against white unions. If the vote of the American Federation of Labor to unionize Negroes was an anticipation and a recognition of the menace of a division of labor along color lines, that state of mind found recognition in the South. For the first time to any marked extent white labor realized the necessity for making allies of colored workers. Any such general change of front by white workmen would menace the very foundations of the color line as it is drawn in the South. It is, therefore, significant to note what extraordinary measures were adopted to prevent a coalition of white and colored labor. As always, the advocates of the color line brought about violence to sustain the division. It is a melodramatic episode which reveals the forces which were at work in the South.

In Bogalusa, Louisiana, on November 22, 1919, three white men were shot dead, and a number were severely wounded. One of the men killed was district president of the American Federation of Labor; another was a union carpenter. The white men were killed, according to reports in the newspapers, because they had walked, armed, down the main street of Bogalusa, protecting with their lives and guns the life of a colored labor organizer. "The black man," says Miss Mary White Ovington,[1] "had dared to organize in a district where organization meant at the least exile, at the most death by lynching." In the town where his white protectors were shot dead for refusing to give him up, the controlling lumber company had in the fall of 1919 ordered twenty-five hundred union men to destroy their union cards. "The company," said Miss Ovington, "has at its command the Loyalty League, a state organization formed during the war, not of soldiers,

[1] *The Liberator*, January, 1920.

but of men at home, part of whose business it was to see that every able-bodied man (Negro understood) should work at any task, at any wage, and for any hours that the employer might desire. They had back of them the state 'work or fight' law and might put to work men temporarily unemployed save that the provision of the Act did not apply to 'persons temporarily unemployed by reasons of differences with their employers such as strikes or lockouts.' Under this legislation it was small wonder that unionism was forbidden by the lumber company; or that, unionism continuing, despite the master's mandate, the Loyalty League, though the war was ended, continued its work." It was in the continuance of this "work" that the Negro organizer was hunted and the three white union men who protected him were shot down.

The account of the affair published in *The New York Times* of November 23, 1919, is worthy of quotation for its frankness:[1]

"Trouble between the Loyalty League, which includes ex-service men *and representative[s] of the Great Southern Lumber Company and other business interests* on the one hand,

[1] Italics mine.

and union labor, . . . on the other, began last night after about five hundred armed members of the League held up a train half a mile from the railroad station and searched it for *undesirables.* After the search had failed to reveal any one *whose presence was unwelcome,* the crowd started to find a Negro who was said to have been active recently in trying to stir up bad feeling among his race against the whites. The search, continued until a late hour, was unsuccessful.

"This morning, to the surprise of the Loyalty League men, the Negro they sought emerged from his hiding-place and walked boldly down the principal street of the town. On either side of him was an armed white man. . . ." In view of the protection of the Negro by white union men, the contention of the Loyalty Leaguers is significant: "They said the black man had been trying to cause race-rioting and that they did not intend to permit him to stay there." It would seem that the black man had been an extraordinary organizer of race riots to enlist white men as his defenders. "Rallying their forces quickly, the Loyalty Leaguers forced the three to retreat to an automobile garage. When called upon to surrender the Negro, the men in the garage refused, and firing began. Williams, Bouchillon, and Gaines sacrificed their lives in protecting the Negro, whose name [Saul Dechus] was not learned, and O'Rourke received fatal wounds." The connection of business and "loyalty" is further indicated in a subsequent despatch, published in *The New York Globe* November 24, 1919, which refers to "members of the 'Loyalty League,' made up partly from the employees of the Great Southern Lumber Company," who "attempted to arrest the Negro."

As early as June, 1919, the president of the New Orleans branch of the National Association for the Advancement of Colored People had reported the expulsion from Bogalusa of respectable colored men, "among them a doctor owning about fifty thousand dollars' worth of property" because they had refused to advise colored people against joining the unions. The committee which visited the colored citizens gave them twenty minutes, or an hour, or six hours, to leave town, according to their circumstances. One of the Negroes, sixty-five years old, who was beaten on the night before the hunt for the Negro organizer which cost four white men's lives, wrote of his experiences to *The New Orleans Vindicator:*

"I moved to Bogalusa in 1907. I worked off and on for the Great Southern Lumber Company up to the time the labor trouble began. In November I met a member of the so-called 'strong-armed squad' and he said to me, 'Why don't you go back to work?' I said that the company demanded that I tear up my union card and that was the only condition under which we would be allowed to go back to work—renounce our union membership and get back into the old rut where we had always been until just a short while ago when we joined the union. He replied to me, 'Well, you had better get out of this town!' I thought little of the remark at first because I have always tried to live peaceable with everybody and, secondly, I could not think that any civilized man in this day and time could think of killing a man because he tried, in a legal way, to get all that he could for his labor. This man proved to be one of the gang that came to my home Friday night and dragged me out and beat me. I know him well and he knows me."

Officers of local labor unions telegraphed to the United States Attorney-General, to the president of the American Federation of

Labor, and to the Secretary of War, recalling their repeated requests for investigation of conditions in Bogalusa. Whatever the outcome of investigation or neglect, one fact of major significance for race relations was uncovered there. As Miss Ovington said in comment, "Not since the days of Populism has the South seen so dramatic an espousal by the white man of the black man's cause." It indicated the beginning of the end of the exploitation of both white and colored workers which had been accomplished by pitting their groups against one another and by fanning the animosities that left them hostile.[1]

The supremacy is menaced of lumber companies which exploit black labor mercilessly by preventing organization. White men, too poor to pay a poll tax, ignorant, and disfranchised, have found a key to such industrial conditions as those in Bogalusa. When they join forces with colored labor a political, as well as an industrial system that is founded in misinformation, oppression, artificially fostered hatreds and brutalities, begins to totter. As the color line is stretched and becomes a matter of national

[1] Further information on the Bogalusa episode is contained in Appendix.

concern, it becomes more and more evident that colored labor cannot be treated as though it were a monstrosity or a rare specimen. Too much evidence is at hand which demonstrates that not only have colored men done their work as well as white, often increasing output in factories manned previously by white men, but also have worked in amity, without friction, among white workers. The elaborate plans made by the steel companies to obtain and to keep Negro labor tell their own story. The Urban League of Pittsburgh found that the Negro laborer "can do anything the white worker can do." If some negroes are unsteady, on the other hand there are "hundreds and hundreds and even thousands of Negroes who have not lost a single day and are counted upon by concerns as their most dependable men." A letter from the head of a Negro welfare association of Cleveland says of a questionnaire sent to employers: "The employers' opinion as to efficiency has been very satisfactory. This is determined by the answers contained in a questionnaire sent out to one hundred and fifty industrial plants. Most of these answers have been returned, but the data have not been compiled. Only two or three, so far, have expressed dissatisfaction, and even their criticism is qualified." A letter from an officer of the Department of Labor states: "Employers of labor have informed me that the Negro is not less efficient than the native white and is more efficient than certain types of foreigners. The charge of inefficiency usually comes from locations where 'camps' obtain or where housing facilities are inadequate. It is unreasonable to expect 100-per-cent. efficiency from a man who is obliged to sleep in a public park, in a sub-basement, in a bathtub, or in a ten-by-twelve-foot room with half a dozen other men."

Dr. George E. Haynes, Director of Negro Economics of the Department of Labor, in a letter of November 12, 1919, quoted the following as "characteristic opinions" of employers. From an automobile firm in Detroit, Michigan: "We have in our employ some twelve hundred to fifteen hundred Negroes. They are giving very satisfactory services."

Another such firm reported the reorganization of one department whose work had been done "by seventy white men of many nationalities, and by working overtime these seventy men were producing an average of eighteen chassis per day. The work included riveting, drilling, filing, and pressing in hangers and bushings. Within six weeks after this department had been reorganized, using Negro workers exclusively, fifty men were producing from forty to fifty assemblies per day, and overtime work had been greatly reduced. This showed a clear increase in efficiency of over 300 per cent."

A news paragraph from the Department of Labor, published early in February, reported a decrease in the accident rate as Negro molders and helpers supplanted other labor in the foundries of Indianapolis: "Another very interesting fact is that both union and non-union white molders have worked with these Negroes in most friendly co-operation. . . . The general testimony of the foundry owners and managers in a number of foundries is that the Negro molders have given entire satisfaction under the strenuous war pace, and that the Negro is making good. *Some managers say that the conditions that exist between workers depend upon the individual and not upon the race.*"[1]

It is not necessary to draw from the evidence presented any conclusions other than

[1] Italics mine.

those written upon the face of the facts—namely, that the Negro has enormously enlarged his sphere of opportunity in industry by doing satisfactorily the work allotted to him; that he has worked with white men amicably; and that the future of the American labor movement will be involved to some extent in the position which the Negro workman is given or takes. In the existing state of industrial organization, the Negro's capabilities, as they may be limited or determined by racial inheritance, play a small part. With few exceptions industries are not so thoroughly organized that slight individual and psychological differences make themselves felt in large-scale production. Meanwhile the test of practice has been applied. The results have shown industrial corporations eager to employ and to retain Negro labor. That is a fact which, regardless of racial prejudice, actual or alleged racial "inferiority," it is necessary for any student of labor currents to take into account.

It was not uncommon during the steel strike of 1919 for such captions to be published as the following in *The New York Tribune* of September 24th, "Race War Feared at Gary Plants—Negroes Imported from Birmingham Stir Anger of the Strikers." The caption was followed by a first paragraph announcing that "threats of a race war between foreign-born strikers and Negro steel men remaining at work drew interest," as more mills were closed. What was described as an "undercurrent of hostility" was explained by the assertion that "three hundred Negroes, recently imported from Birmingham, Alabama, refused to heed the call of the union and remained at work, keeping fires under the furnaces of the Indiana Steel Company." "It is unfortunate," says Mr. Epstein, "that often a race issue is made of a purely labor question."

It has been charged that at various times deliberate attempts have been made to foment racial antagonisms, not only against Negroes, but against and among "foreigners" in order to divide labor and make organization difficult, if not impossible. On November 2d a despatch attributed to the Universal News Service quoted "State-Attorney Hoyne" as saying that steel-mills of the Chicago district had employed a detective agency to foment violence during the strike. Complaint against the agency had been made by Edward N. Nockels, secretary of the Chicago Federation of Labor, who "charged the concern employed scores of men throughout the steel district, who were instructed to create race hatred between Negroes and whites and urge workmen to violence." Mr. Hoyne was quoted as having said: "There is no doubt in my mind that the —— Service, through its operatives, was engaged in stirring up riots. Its operatives destroyed or advocated the destruction of property, aroused antagonism between different groups of strikers, and employed sluggers. The agency admitted that it was employed by the Steel and Tube Company of America, but they deny knowledge of the methods of the concern."

Much of the mistaken "Americanization" propaganda conducted by influential newspapers endeavored to create an issue of industrial "loyalty" as between American-born workers who stood by their companies and foreign-born workers who joined unions and struck. Not infrequently, in the course of such realignments, it was discovered that the Negro was a real "American" and the foreign-born white man was the alien. In this play of industrial forces the status of racial groups was relative to purely economic motives. In the South it is the Negro who is alien. In the North the Negro is often "American," as opposed to those who would be considered his superiors south of the Ohio River. The dangers are obvious of such irresponsible industrial leadership as seeks to control labor through hatreds and ignorance. These dangers would be obvious, even if there were not Atlanta, East St. Louis, and Chicago to stand as dramatic warnings. That the Negro has come to realize how closely his status is bound up with equality of industrial opportunity there is abundant testimony. Mr. Carl Sandburg points out that "it is economic equality that gets the emphasis in the speeches and the writings of the colored people themselves." And he lists the new doors of opportunity which were opened to Negroes in Chicago in the two years preceding the Chicago riots of 1919, among them foundries, tanneries, freight-warehouses, automobile-repair shops, a mattress-factory, gas-meter inspectorships. The Negro has been engaged in conquering and making his own new industrial fields. That development was bound to come in time. It was undoubtedly accelerated by the World War, as much as fifty years, in the estimation of a number of observers. One fruit of the acceleration was acute conflict which came of the same sort of maladjustment that attended the influx of immigrant labor from abroad. What fostered the violence and the industrial riots of 1919, some of them erroneously called race riots, was the unduly sensitive, in fact, morbid, state of the public mind with regard to color. It rests very largely with labor, white and colored, whether the divisions that have caused havoc are to be perpetuated and made irreconcilable. The broadest path toward harmonization of racial differences in the future lies in labor organization. As soon as a community of interest is recognized between white and colored workers, as it was recognized in the heart of the South, in Bogalusa, Louisiana, race prejudice fades into its proper place as a bogy, a set of ungoverned and unanalyzed emotions, which can be stimulated to the detriment of the people who harbor those emotions. In more than one place the color line is being swept irresistibly out of labor organizations.

"We all know there are unions in the American Federation of Labor that have their feet in the twentieth century and their heads in the sixteenth century," said the secretary of the Stockyards Labor Council of Chicago, according to Mr. Sandburg. The same investigator quotes one of the officers of a packing company as saying: "In the yards it is not a race question at all. It is a labor-union question!" The question is still debated whether the Negro is or is not a "good union man." In fact, the Negro was and has been shown to be systematically discriminated against, until the industrial weight of his numbers and his competence made itself felt. If many Negroes are not now good union men, it is because they have never, despite their interest and their desire, been given opportunity to have an effective part in the American labor movement.

II

Housing

What was mainly a labor and an industrial readjustment on a large scale during and immediately following the World War was complicated by the absence of plans for decently housing the immigrants. As Mr. Epstein has shown of Pittsburgh, the bulk of Negro laborers who came North fell between the ages of eighteen and forty. Rents were abnormally high and the large number of unmarried men lived under unsanitary conditions. Thus, of 390 Negroes Mr. Epstein examined, 57 lived in rooms housing more than 6 people and 98 in rooms occupied by 4 persons. Of conditions in rooming-houses, Mr. Epstein noted that 13 per cent. of the men without families, who came under his observation, slept three or more in one bed, and "in many instances, houses in which these rooms are located are dilapidated dwellings with the paper torn off, the plaster sagging from the naked lath, the windows broken, the ceiling low and damp, and the whole room dark, stuffy, and unsanitary." Some of the rooms "with more than six people sleeping in them at one time have practically no openings for either light or air." In Chicago, as elsewhere, the planlessness with which Northern industrial cities met the Southern Negro occasioned overcrowding, and an overflow of the Negro residence district. Branded as an alien and an interloper, the Negro was also made to seem an invader of white residence districts. "Most of the Negro workmen," said *The*

New York Tribune in its despatch warning of industrial conflict about Gary, "live in a section of the city adjoining that of the foreign element, and bitterness has been manifested since the first call of the walkout." Mr. Sandburg listed housing as the first of three "radical and active factors," in any American city where the racial situation was critical.

Antagonism against competing labor is easily made to accompany hatred of alien neighbors. In Chicago the influx of Negroes was accompanied by aggressive propaganda in the newspapers and in meetings, many of them held secretly, urging white men to stand firm against the "invasion" of their districts by Negroes. Undoubtedly it was to the advantage of certain real-estate speculators to create a state of mind bordering on panic among property-owners. Property was sold at abnormally low prices and immediately thereafter rose in value. Of the so-called Black Belt in Chicago, Mr. Sandburg wrote: "There seem to be certain preposterous axioms of real-estate exchange governing this district and no others in Chicago. These axioms might be stated thus:

"(1) Sell at a loss and the rent goes higher, and

"(2) The larger the number of colored persons ready to pay higher rentals the lower the realty values slump."

In this peculiar game the Negro was as much a victim as he was in the contest of capital and labor. Bombing of Negro residences during the early months of 1919 was variously attributed to "race feeling" and to the conflict of rival real-estate interests. The question of politics was also raised when the bombings were referred to as part of a campaign to terrorize the Negro out of settling and becoming a political power in the Third as well as in the Second Ward. In at least one case a bomb was exploded, not in the Negro district, but in front of the house of a white real-estate owner who had been warned to get rid of Negro tenants on his property.

The industrial implications of inadequate housing for Negro migrants were emphasized in various ways. For the congestion and consequent overflow of the Chicago Negro-residence district the packing and other companies which had imported colored workers were partly responsible. Yet, although the dangerous effects of the encroachment of colored residents upon white districts were repeatedly pointed out, no intelligent effort was made to provide homes for the colored people. To the bitterness felt and expressed by union men of Chicago was added the panic of property-owners. "The profiteering meat-packers of Chicago," said John Fitzpatrick of the Chicago Federation of Labor, "are responsible for the race riots which have disgraced our city. It is the outcome of their deliberate attempt to disrupt the union-labor movement in the yards" (*Chicago Tribune*, August 18, 1919).

Yet these riots were almost universally spoken of in connection with housing. As early as July 13th, weeks before the outbreak occurred, *The Chicago Herald-Examiner* published an account of a suit for damages brought against a property-owners' association by a Negro whose property had been bombed. Four "real-estate men" connected with the Kenwood Property Owners' Association were made defendants of the suit and the plaintiff's attorney asserted that "the men who placed the bomb are in the employ of real-estate men to frighten Negroes out of Kenwood." As late as October, 1919, the anti-Negro propaganda found expression in a mass-meeting of two thousand persons under the auspices of the Kenwood and Hyde Park Property Owners' Association. The treasurer of the organization "precipitated the climax of the meeting when he requested all who would work to free the district of Negroes to stand up. With one accord, every man and woman arose with shouts" (*Chicago Herald-Examiner*, October 21, 1919). The threatened "Negro influx" in the white residential district about Michigan, Calumet, and Vincent Avenues and Grand Boulevard assumed a different complexion when a Negro lawyer, representing a committee of Negro residents, explained that colored people would willingly enough leave white districts "if suitable quarters and reasonable rentals could be provided any place in the city where the Negroes could be to themselves" (*Chicago Herald-Examiner*, October 25, 1919). "The interchange of ideas took place frankly and in a friendly spirit," at this meeting, and, when the meeting adjourned, "a vote of thanks was tendered the Negroes for their spirit of fairness and open-mindedness" (*Chicago Tribune*, October 25, 1919).

J. Gray Lucas, representing the colored

residents, intelligently and simply formulated the problems before the meeting. "The white man controls capital and regulates values," he was quoted as saying. "If your property values go down, it is your own fault. If a Negro family moves into a white block, every one else sacrifices his interests in a panic and runs away. You ask what you can do for the colored man. You must offer him a better place to live at a more reasonable price than he is now paying. Then he will be glad to move. He does not invade the white district because he wants white neighbors, but simply because he wants the most comfort and the best home he can get for his money."

The trouble which had originated in Chicago's industrial *laissez-faire*, which had been inflated to a grotesque menace by real-estate speculators, by honest but stupid panic due to the press, by political greed, and a small residue of malevolence, seemed here to have been brought into some sort of light. For property-owners, as for labor-unionists, it was made glaringly evident that color and the habits of thought which come from emphasizing color distinctions must be subordinated to the need for joint consideration of common difficulties. For white folk to talk of segregating the Negro is to invite disabilities and difficulties for themselves in American cities. Even such an influx of Negro immigrants as war industry brought to Chicago could be considered and dealt with, not in the fashion of big stick and repression, but in open meeting and frank discussion. The conclusion which has been pointed for white labor is no less plain than that which stared Chicago's property-owners in the face.

Not only the Negro's position in industry, but the orderliness with which new forms of society are devised, depends upon the Negro's sense of his real share in the building of American civilization. He has been by force of circumstance inducted into the technical and social complexities of industrialism. He may be made a valuable source of power and inventiveness, or he may be driven to the self-defense which means destruction of the society which provokes it. The housing problem occasioned by the immigration to Northern cities was incidental to a rapid change. It brought the residents of cities up to a set of problems that labor-unionists and industrialists had already begun to formulate for themselves.

VIII

THE AMERICAN CONGO

IT will be many years, perhaps, before the story of the "freed" Negro in the Southern states is written down intelligibly, trimmed of the animosity which imputes to Northern commercialism or to Southern aristocracy an undue burden of responsibility for oppression. In a time when race questions are being furiously agitated, when a northward migration is in progress and the political scene vibrates to the mention or thought of color, interpretation becomes hazardous. It is possible, however, to sift the miscellany that masquerades as news and to begin clearing the sadly blotted and obscured record. A detached mind, unacquainted with historical, economic, or emotional determinants, entering upon such a task, and taking American professions at something like face value, could not fail to find conditions prevailing in 1920 so sadly at variance with current conceptions of Americanism or civilization as almost to deprive the words of their meaning. Innumerable brutalities have been set down in glaring letters against white and black men. But it is the white men who avowedly dominate; their press creates the popular sentiment which sets the cultural tone of the South; it is the white man's courts and the white man's juries which administer law; it is, finally, white soldiers whose bullets and bayonets are called for to preserve or to restore order. In the circumstances, one step toward setting the record clear would consist in an examination of the white man's records and processes for signs of chronic racial maladjustment; for such maladjustment can be shown endemic in many of the Southern states, and not only expresses itself dramatically and tragically, but occasions the diffusion of race problems over the entire land. However true it is that floods or the plague of boll weevils in Southwestern cotton-fields starved out Negroes, it was still the Negro's position in society, the treatment accorded him as producer and as human being which impelled him to go North. "The treatment accorded the Negro always stood second, when not first, among the reasons given by Negroes for leaving the South," wrote Mr. W. T. B. Williams.[1] "I talked with all classes of colored people from Virginia to Louisiana—farm-hands, tenants, farmers, hack-drivers, porters, mechanics, barbers, merchants, insurance men, teachers, heads of schools, ministers, druggists, physicians, and lawyers—and in every instance the matter of treatment came to the front voluntarily. This is the all-absorbing, burning question among Negroes. For years no group of the thoughtful, intelligent class of Negroes, at any rate, have met for any purpose without finally drifting into some discussion of their treatment at the hands of white people." It would be possible to draw up an indictment of that treatment by emphasizing isolated brutalities, such as the burning at stake of fourteen colored men in the United States in the year 1919. The details of many lynchings have seared the pages on which they were described and could again be made to evoke a thrill of horror from readers. But the record demands not stories of horror alone; it requires some exposition of motive. Violence is merely

[1] Report of W. T. B. Williams, *Negro Migration in 1916–17*. U.S. Department of Labor.

a means to an end, even if that end be the glutting of passion.

In any civilization where questions of personal freedom were so closely bound to economic considerations as in the pre-Civil War South, those economic considerations were bound to exert influence even when apparently the connection had been broken. The endeavor to keep the Negro in economic subjection through the enactment of the "Black Codes" is now an old story. Yet old stories repeat themselves. "The report of the Attorney-General for the year 1907 contains a list of eighty-three complaints of peonage pending in the Department of Justice," says Mr. Lafayette M. Hershaw.[1] It is worth while to quote Justice Brewer's definition of peonage as it is given by Mr. Hershaw: "It may be defined as a status or condition of compulsory service based upon the indebtedness of the peon to the master. The basal fact is indebtedness. One fact exists universally, all were indebted to their masters. This was the cord by which they seemed bound to their masters' service." "Therefore," comments Mr. Hershaw,

[1] Lafayette M. Hershaw, *Peonage.* Occasional Papers, No. 15. The American Negro Academy. Washington, 1915.

"wherever we have compulsory service for debt we have peonage, it matters not by what method the result is obtained." The definition is pertinent in view of a letter published in *The Memphis Commercial Appeal*, early in 1919, and signed "A Southerner."

"In certain parts of the South," says the writer, "men who consider themselves men of honor and would exact a bloody expiation of one who would characterize them as common cheats do not hesitate to boast that they rob the Negroes by purchasing their cotton at prices that are larcenous, by selling goods to them at extortionate figures, and even by padding their accounts *with a view of keeping them always in debt.* A protest from a Negro against tactics of this kind is met with a threat of force. Justice at the hands of a white jury in sections where this practice obtains is inconceivable. Even an attempt to carry the matter into the courts is usually provocative of violence."

"Apparently, in order to secure his labor," says Mr. W. T. B. Williams of the farm tenant in Mississippi, "the landlord often will not settle for the year's work till late in the spring when the next crop has been 'pitched.' The Negro is then bound hand

and foot and must accept the landlord's terms. It usually means that it is impossible for him to get out of the landlord's clutches, no matter how he is being treated. In many cases the Negro does not dare ask for a settlement." And later Mr. Williams remarks: "The beating of farm-hands on the large plantations in the lower South is so common that many colored people look upon every great plantation as a peon camp; and in sawmills and other public works it is not at all unusual for bosses to knock Negroes around with pieces of lumber or anything else that happens to come handy." A condition of servitude and oppression is testified to by a number of observers. Against this dark background a lurid illumination was thrown from the riots which occurred in Phillips County, Arkansas, in October of 1919. As most phases of the strained relations between the races have eventuated in violence, so the exploitation of Negro farm tenants was bound to produce it.

Following closely upon the sacking of the court-house in Omaha, Nebraska, with the barely unsuccessful attempt to hang the mayor, the affray which occurred on September 30th in a small Arkansas town and provoked conflict between white and colored men did not at first attract much attention. In the ensuing days, to October 6th, more and more alarming reports shocked the country into wakefulness. What was first described as a race riot became a "revolt," an "uprising," a plot by Negroes to "massacre all whites." "All Whites Marked for Slaughter," announced a scarehead of *The New York Evening Telegram* on October 6th. *The New York Times* followed suit with "Planned Massacre of Whites To-day." *The New York Tribune* announced "Negro Plot to Massacre All Whites Found." *The Memphis Commercial Appeal* found that "Negroes Had Planned General Slaughter" and *The Arkansas Gazette* had blazoned the assertions that "Vicious Blacks Were Planning Great Uprising—All Evidence Points to Carefully Planned Rebellion." Rebellion, revolt, insurrection, massacre, plot, night-riding, "Negro Paul Reveres"—every word that might suggest the clandestine, the violent, the menacing, was lavishly used to describe conditions in Arkansas. Throughout the United States the impression was created by Associated Press despatches and by numerous correspondents that Negroes had organized against white men and had planned to murder and to rob.

A town called Hoop Spur, but a few miles from the Mississippi River and some twenty-five miles southwest of Helena, was the scene of the initial outbreak. A shooting affray had taken place here between Negroes assembled in a country church and two white men with a Negro prisoner in an automobile outside. The white men, W. A. Adkins, a "special agent" for the Missouri Pacific Railroad, and Charles Pratt, deputy sheriff, were said to be on their way to arrest a "white bootlegger" or whisky-smuggler, who had been causing trouble in Elaine. The white men, it was asserted, "had trouble with their car" and stopped just outside the Negro church (*Arkansas Gazette*, October 4th). There would seem to be a strong element of coincidence in the automobile trouble which would halt a white deputy sheriff on a country road just outside a church in which a meeting of Negroes was being held. From that point accounts differ. The white press asserted that the meeting had been maturing its conspiracy plot, and suspected that their plans had been discovered. The Negroes, it was asserted, "opened fire, killing Adkins, and severely wounding Pratt." A despatch from Helena, of October 5th, credited to the Associated Press, spoke of the widespread uprising which had been planned, and asserted that at Hoop Spur "there were one hundred armed Negroes in the church at the scene of the shooting," of whom some were said to be women "carrying automatic revolvers in their stockings" (*Arkansas Gazette*, October 6, 1919). Fifty thousand rounds of ammunition were announced as having been found in the Branch Normal School, a colored institution of Pine Bluff. A subsequent despatch on October 6th, inconspicuously printed, explained that the ammunition had been sent there by the government for the training of student officers during the World War, and the store had been found intact. But the initial report of the finding of the ammunition, the Associated Press reported, had led "authorities here to believe the contemplated uprising was of more than a local nature, possibly planned for the entire South" (*Arkansas Gazette*, October 6th).

Panic rumor spread. The country-side was roused. The Governor of Arkansas called for United States troops. White planters and their friends organized themselves into posses and a hunt for "niggers" began. Fighting took place in Elaine, next to Hoop Spur, where armed white men maintained headquarters. No accurate record was kept of the number of colored men killed, "but according to one member of the posse from Helena, who came in from the scene of the fighting late yesterday, 'there are plenty of them'" (*Arkansas Democrat*, October 2, 1919). "Possemen from various towns, after numerous clashes with Negroes yesterday afternoon, had gathered at Elaine to spend the night," said the same newspaper; furthermore "the white women in the town were concentrated in the center of the town and all white men stayed on guard throughout the night." "Wild rumors," reported *The Arkansas Gazette* of October 8th, "were abroad in Helena last night to the effect that Negroes were armed 'somewhere' and would attack the outlying homes during the night. Investigation revealed no foundation for these rumors." Harry Cherry, correspondent of *The Memphis Press*, reported on October 4th that he had followed "posses and soldiers into the canebrakes in search of Negro desperadoes who were defying the officers." He reported having seen dead bodies lying in the road not far from Helena, and noted further, "Enraged citizens fired at the bodies of the dead Negroes as they road [rode] out of Helena toward Elaine. . . ." "Every one of the five hundred troops who went to Elaine appeared anxious to get into battle with the blacks," reported a correspondent of an Arkansas newspaper of October 6th. A despatch to *The Arkansas Gazette* of October 3d, headed "Lynching Discussed?" reported a meeting of Helena business men at the court-house, from which newspaper correspondents had been excluded. "It was said that a probable or threatened lynching was discussed."

Under the circumstances it seems a euphemism to compliment the white people of Phillips County, Arkansas, on the absence of race hatred among them and to speak of their calm behavior and willingness to let the law take its course, as did Mr. Jack C. Wilson, executive secretary of the Mississippi Welfare League, who had come to see how race relations were administered in Arkansas. Meanwhile, white men were being armed throughout the county and Negroes disarmed. "More than three hundred special deputy sheriffs [white] were sworn in by Sheriff Kitchens and sent to the scene of the insurrection" (*Arkansas Gazette*, October 6th). Canebrakes in the low-lying lands were searched for Negroes who had fled, and soldiers "were instructed to permit any black to surrender, but to shoot to kill if they showed any inclination to fight" (*Arkansas Gazette*, October 6th). Furthermore, all Negroes in the vicinity of the trouble were required to show passes signed by army officers, and these passes "were issued only when the Negroes' employers would vouch for them." This fact assumes extraordinary significance when it is known that the relations of employer and farm-hand, of landlord and tenant were at the root of the Phillips County "massacre." For it meant that the employers, or landlords, parties to the trouble, were given what under the circumstances was the enormous power of sanctioning or declining to sanction the free movement of their employees or tenants.

White Mississippians took the opportunity for improving their methods, to come to Arkansas for study. "County officials and other representatives from various towns and counties in Mississippi, including Friar's Point on the river, Clarksdale, Cleveland, Tunica, Greenwood, Sumner, and Charleston, were here to-day conferring with the Committee of Seven as to the methods employed in dealing with the troubles in this county" (*Arkansas Gazette*, October 8th). It will be seen that the conditions which prevailed in Phillips County, Arkansas, before the disturbance must have had points of similarity to the state of affairs in other parts of the South, notably Mississippi. What was the explanation of those conditions as it was given by white men?

A committee of seven white men, apparently self-constituted, but "authorized" by the Governor of Arkansas to investigate the disorders in Phillips County, published a statement through one of its members, E. M. Allen, president of the Helena Business Men's League and "owner of considerable property" (*Chicago Tribune*, October 7th). He asserted that the trouble in Phillips County had been not a race riot, but "a deliberately planned insurrection of the Negroes against the whites, directed by an organization known as the Progressive Farmers' and Household Union of America, *established for the sole purpose of banding Negroes together for the killing of white people.*" Especial emphasis is to be given this statement, coming as it does from a "leading business man" and an "owner of considerable property." Formation of the Farmers' Union Mr. Allen attributed to Robert L. Hill, "a Negro, twenty-six years of age, of Winchester, Arkansas, who saw in it an opportunity of 'easy money.'" Hill first organized a lodge at Ratio "because his mother happened to be living there." He was charged by Mr. Allen with representing himself to the Negroes as an agent of the federal government deputized to call the organization into existence. "The slogan of the organization is, 'We battle for our rights!'" Hill was charged with extorting membership fees from ignorant and credulous colored people. *The Chicago Tribune's* caption described the Phillips County riots as "The Harebrained Plot of a Negro Wallingford—Amazing Story of Scheme to Slay All Whites of Arkansas Bared." At least two white men were said to have assisted in the organization of the Progressive Farmers' and Household Union of America, one of them being O. S. Bratton of Little Rock, Arkansas, who, according to *The Arkansas Democrat* of October 3d, was "charged with murder in connection with the death of W. A. Adkins," shot outside the Negro church at Hoop Spur.

In an article in *The Memphis Press* of October 4th O. S. Bratton was described as "a Little Rock lawyer who had been prominent in Republican politics," and he was said to be "charged with being implicated in the murder of O. R. Lilly, real-estate man, and also with incensing the blacks." "In a calmer mood," reported *The Arkansas Gazette* of the same day, "the feeling of bitterness against Bratton seemed to have somewhat diminished, and it is said that the nature of the documents found in his possession had no direct bearing on the action of the insurgent Negroes, although they might have had some influence in that direction." Nevertheless, in the first heat of panic, O. S. Bratton had been charged with murder and "brought to Helena in chains" (*Arkansas Democrat*, October 2d). "Feeling against him is bitter, but there has so far been no indication of summary action." The charge of murder and incitement to riot evaporated when the grand jury of Phillips County indicted O. S. Bratton on a charge of barratry or inciting unnecessary lawsuits, and this dangerous agitator, murderer, and insurrectionist was released on his own recognizances.

The case as it was stated against the

Negroes of Phillips County has been given in some detail. They were insurrectionists and had planned a massacre of white men. Their "Progressive Farmers' and Household Union of America" was formed for that sole purpose by a Negro named Hill, who had misrepresented his position and hoped to profit from their credulity. The plans of the organization as they were represented in the white press varied from the slaughter of every white man in the state of Arkansas to the taking over of the land in Phillips County. White men were implicated and were accused of having assisted the Negroes in organizing. One of the white men was brought to Helena in chains, charged unofficially with murder, but subsequently released under a perfunctory indictment for barratry. Meanwhile, at least five white men and twenty-five Negroes had been killed in the turmoil. In the case against the Negroes as it appeared in the white press, there were, however, certain discrepancies. Thus, of the meeting of Negroes in the church at Hoop Spur, *The Memphis Commercial Appeal* of October 3d remarked that "the Negroes were meeting in this church Tuesday night, *as is their custom. . . .*" Despite the assertion of E. M. Allen that the Farmers' Union had been established "for the sole purpose of banding Negroes together for the killing of white people," certain other purposes appeared in the news despatches. "With October 6th set as the day for the uprising," reported *The New York Globe* of October 6th, "Negro prisoners are said to have confessed, each member of the organization at specified places was to take a bale of cotton by that date to certain prominent landowners, plantation-managers, and merchants and demand a settlement"—in other words, a statement of account. It will be recalled that denial of "settlements," or statements of account, was one of the means referred to by which Negroes were kept in debt and in a condition closely approximating peonage. Further light is thrown on the situation by a statement attributed to U. S. Bratton, father of the man who was brought to Helena in chains (*Memphis Commercial Appeal*, October 3d). U. S. Bratton had held a number of federal offices, including that of Assistant United States Attorney and postmaster. Mr. Bratton said a Negro from Ratio, Arkansas, had asked Mr. Bratton's law firm to represent him and a number of other Negroes. It was arranged that the son, O. S. Bratton, was to meet the Negroes "and to get the facts from all of them as they claimed them to be, after which we would take the matter up with the manager and see if some amicable settlement could not be made." He found that the Negroes were claiming "that it had been impossible for them to obtain itemized statements of accounts, or in fact to obtain statements at all, and that the manager was preparing to ship their cotton (they being share-croppers and having a half-interest therein) off without settling with them or allowing them to sell their half of the crop and pay up their accounts. As we were informed, there were some sixty-five or seventy of these share-croppers who desired us to represent them. If it's a crime to represent people in an effort to make honest settlements, then he [O. S. Bratton] has committed a crime. If this is a crime in a country where we have been spending our money and the lives of our boys to make the country safe for democracy, we do not understand what the word means. The above are facts which a full investigation will show beyond the peradventure of a doubt, and we court the fullest investigation." U. S. Bratton being a reputable lawyer of

Arkansas, albeit a Republican in Democratic territory, his statement strengthens the supposition that the Negroes of Ratio, at least, had some other motive than massacring their white landlords. Despite the confident assertions of Arkansas white men as to the purposes of the Progressive Farmers' and Household Union of America, published quotations from the literature of the organization indicated none but peaceable intentions. Thus the object of the union was to be "to advance the interests of the Negro, mentally and intellectually, and to make him a better citizen and a better farmer" (*Arkansas Gazette*, October 6th). The articles of incorporation of the union had been drawn "by Williamson and Williamson of Monticello, white men and ex-slaveholders" (Walter F. White in *The Nation*, December 6th). In this connection it is significant that the Committee of Seven found among the "ringleaders" of the movement "the oldest and most reliable of the Negroes whom we have known for the past fifteen years." It would have been strange, indeed, if these men had lent themselves to a conspiracy "to put to death a dozen or more prominent white men, seize the land, and generally take over control of the country," as the Committee of Seven charged (Associated Press Despatch, November 2d). Apparently the open inquiry courted by U. S. Bratton was not to take place. As Negro prisoners were brought into Helena from the stockade in which they had been confined in Elaine, plans were made to interrogate them. "It is now believed," said *The Arkansas Gazette* of October 8th, "that no open hearings of the cases against the men and women charged with participating in the insurrection will be held. There are more than three hundred separate cases to be investigated, and it is believed that the hearings can be expedited if held privately."

The court proceedings during the trial of the Negro insurrectionists, in the course of which five colored men were found guilty of murder in the first degree by a white jury in seven minutes, are matters which might well claim a separate chapter. "It took the jury eight minutes to return a verdict against Frank Hicks," said *The Memphis Commercial Appeal* of November 4th, "charged with the murder of Clinton Lee, a citizen of Helena, near Hoop Spur on the morning of October 1st. Hicks was found 'guilty as charged in the indictment,' the verdict automatically sending him to the electric chair. But that record was broken in the gathering afternoon darkness when a jury retired at 5.32 to decide the fate of five other Negroes charged with the murder of Lee. Seven minutes later they returned a verdict finding the defendants guilty, sending them to the electric chair." It will be recalled that the trials of Negro farmers were held, without change of venue, in the very county in which the disorders had occurred, by juries composed of white men, from which Negroes were excluded. One colored man was sentenced to twenty-one years in the penitentiary. He had been charged with first-degree murder. "Material witnesses on the murder charge were absent," said *The Arkansas Gazette* of November 8th, "and the court allowed the defendant to plead guilty to second-degree murder. The only witness to the murder of Corporal Earls is an officer recently discharged from the army, who could not be located in time for the trial." It is almost unbelievable that in the United States a man could be convicted and sentenced to twenty-one years in prison without any witness appearing against him. Under the circumstances it is not astonishing that the defendant agreed to plead guilty to second-degree murder as an alternative to being sent to the electric chair. A correspondent of *The Memphis Commercial Appeal* reported on November 5th, when forty-eight colored men had been convicted, of whom eleven were sentenced to death, "Progress was not as rapid as expected because many Negroes hesitated before pleading guilty to the charge of second-degree murder, a compromise offered by the state." The despatch is full of matter which reveals the way of white juries in Arkansas with Negro defendants: "The first four Negroes arraigned at the afternoon session . . . pleaded not guilty when the state offered to compromise with them if they would admit guilt to a second-degree charge. 'Call a jury,' the court ordered, but before a jury was organized the Negroes changed their minds. They pleaded guilty to a charge of murder in the second degree and were sentenced to twenty-one years in the penitentiary." At one point in the trials "after Judge Jackson had sentenced twenty-four Negroes for five years each," the district attorney "arose and objected," saying: "I do not think these Negroes are receiving sufficient punishment. These Negroes all were at the home of Frank Moore, armed and waiting." In the offhand fashion of Arkansas trial procedure, the judge replied, "I think five years is enough," and the arraignments continued. Unconscious irony laid its light touch on the despatch when the correspondent remarked, toward the close, "Expressions of regret over the necessity of condemning so large a number of Negroes is [*sic*] heard daily on the streets of the city and in the court-room." The master touch, however, was attributed by *The Arkansas Gazette* of November 12th to Judge Jackson. The reader will recall that no Negroes were included in the jury which was convicting colored men of murder. "Frank Moore," said the court, "you have been declared guilty *by a jury of your own choosing* of murder in the first degree. . . ." Judge Jackson denied new trials to the twelve Negroes who had been sentenced to die by electrocution. But the Governor of Arkansas postponed the executions in order to allow appeals to be filed in their behalf. A petition for *habeas corpus*, prepared for filing in the event that that should be necessary, in the federal district court in behalf of Frank Moore, one of the condemned men, draws together a number of the threads of this narrative. The petition, after reciting that plantation-owners had not only declined to give share-croppers itemized statements of their indebtedness for supplies purchased from plantation stores and refused to let the share-croppers dispose of their crops, "but themselves sell and dispose of the same at such prices as they please, and then give to the Negroes no account thereof, in this way keeping them down, poverty-stricken, and under their control." Learning of the employment of Mr. U. S. Bratton as attorney by Negroes of a neighboring plantation, the petitioner and his associates "decided to hold a meeting with the view of seeing him while there, and engaging him as an attorney to protect their interests." While they were assembled in their church, "parties from the outside commenced shooting in the house, through the windows, fired many shots, shot out the lights, and shot one of the members, all of whom, so far as petitioner knows, were unarmed." The church was subsequently burned by armed white men, "thus destroying the indubitable evidence of the assault upon said society." The petitioner asserts that he and other colored prisoners were frequently taken before the Committee of Seven "and were tortured both by whipping, beating, the application of electricity and strangling drugs to compel them to admit guilt which did not exist and to testify against each other; that this torturing was a frequent occurrence, many scars from which petitioner still bears upon his body . . ." and that before the "body called the grand jury, composed exclusively of white men," the petitioner and other Negro prisoners were frequently carried "in an effort to extract from them false incriminating admissions and to testify against each other, and that both before and after they were frequently whipped and tortured. . . ." The men in charge of the prisoners, this petition continues, "had some way of learning when the evidence given or statements made was unsatisfactory to the grand jury, and this was always followed by beating and whipping." The attorney appointed by the court to defend the petitioner "did not consult with him or the other defendants, took no steps to prepare for their defense, asked nothing about their witnesses. . . ." The trial "closed, so far as the evidence was concerned, with the state's witnesses alone"; and the jury "retired just long enough to write a verdict of guilty of murder in the first degree, as charged, and returned with it—not being out exceeding from three to five minutes; the whole proceeding, from beginning to end, occupied about three-fourths of an hour. . . ." There are certain statements in the petition for *habeas corpus* which might have been hearsay, but they were doubtless verifiable by the petitioner's attorney. Thus, it is stated that it had been the practice of thirty years' standing not to choose Negroes to serve on juries, "notwithstanding the Negro population there exceeds the white population by more than five to one, and that a large proportion of them [Negroes] are electors and possess the legal, moral, and intellectual qualifications required or necessary for jurors; that the exclusion of said Negroes from the juries was at all times intentional, and because of their color, of their being Negroes; that such was the case of the grand jury by which petitioner and his co-defendants were indicted, and of the petit jury that pronounced them guilty."[1] The narrative of what occurred in Phillips County, Arkansas, in October of the year 1919 would

[1] Substantially the same facts were recited in a brief filed in the Supreme Court of Arkansas petitioning for a new trial for Frank Moore and other Negroes.

be incomplete without some reference to the white attorney, U. S. Bratton, and his two sons, Capt. Guy G. Bratton and O. S. Bratton, who were so prominently identified in press reports with the "Negro insurrection." Mr. Bratton[1] asked of Senator Charles Curtis of Kansas that a federal investigation be undertaken of affairs in Phillips County. In explanation of his request he recited three circumstances: "(1) My name and family have been brought into and charged with being responsible for the recent troubles in Phillips County, Arkansas. One of my sons, O. S. Bratton, without reason therefor, came near being lynched, having been, without any reason therefor, arrested and kept in jail for thirty-one days, without any examination, or without opportunity being given for bail, or without even being informed of the charge held against him, and where it was asserted that a resort to the time-honored writ of *habeas corpus* to secure his release would result in his being murdered.

"(2) That a deliberate plot was laid to murder one of my sons, namely, Captain Guy G. Bratton, who had recently returned from France, where he had served as a cap-

[1] Copy of memorandum furnished me by Mr. Bratton.

tain, being Division Intelligence Officer of the 87th Division, and who had never even been in Phillips County since his return from the army and his discharge.

"(3) That it was publicly asserted that if I dared to enter the county of Phillips that I would be shot down; this near-lynching, plot to murder and threat against my life being for no reason other than the fact that I had dared to take the cases of poor, unfortunate Negroes, who were being deliberately and systematically robbed of the fruits of their labor." Mr. Bratton, speaking as a Southerner—"my parents and my grandparents were likewise Southerners"—makes the unqualified statement that "the conditions that affect the colored man to-day in the South are even worse than they were before the Civil War. . . . The system of exploitation which goes on is such that the large majority of the Negroes work year in and year out without receiving anything except a scant and bare living. This system is so generally practised that the unfortunate Negroes are absolutely helpless to protect themselves."

During his experience as Assistant United States Attorney, Mr. Bratton recites, "information came to us that peonage was being practised in parts of the state; that certain parties . . . had gone into the state of Texas and had transported a large number of Negro families to their plantations in Arkansas; that the Negroes were unable to get any settlement; that they were unable to get any statements of accounts, other than a small slip of paper upon which were written the words 'balance due'; and that it was contended that any of these tenants, all of whom it was claimed were indebted to these parties, who undertook to leave the state, or, in fact, to leave the premises of these plantation-owners, were guilty of violation of the law." After an investigation by a special agent of the Department of Justice, "warrants were issued for the offending parties and full investigations had before the United States grand jury, resulting in the indictment of the parties and their entering pleas of 'guilty' and paying fines. These facts will all be brought out by an examination of the records of the Department of Justice, to whom the reports were duly made." Open prosecution of tenants for leaving farms has ceased. However, the landlords "accomplish the same result in a different way." One of the means by which the system is maintained is "a private understanding which the planters have among themselves that one will not take a Negro coming from another's plantation who is indebted to the landlord from whose place he is coming, unless he, the landlord who is receiving him, is willing to pay the amount it is claimed by the other landlord is due him." The so-called share-cropper system Mr. Bratton describes as follows: "When the Negroes start in the spring to make a crop, they are to be supplied with groceries and other necessaries of life, to enable them to make a crop. The planters in the majority of cases have what is called 'commissary stores,' from which these supplies are furnished. The articles are furnished at whatever prices the planters and managers see fit to place them, the share-cropper being absolutely helpless, as he has nothing upon which to go and cannot go anywhere else to secure supplies, and hence his only recourse is to walk up to the commissary store and take whatever is dished out to him without any hesitation or question. At the time that this is done, he is not permitted to have any statement or bill of the articles purchased, but must permit the commissary-keeper to enter whatever figures he sees fit to enter. Matters go on in this way until the crops are laid by, then no more supplies are furnished. The Negroes are then required to 'rustle' for subsistence until the gathering-time, when they will again be permitted in some cases to have their half of the money coming from the sale of the cotton seed. When they call for a settlement, they are furnished with a small slip, simply stating 'balance due' so much." Mr. Bratton's report is voluminous. Case after case is cited, with names, dates, and every sort of circumstantial detail. "As to the limits [to] which the plantation-managers will go before they will allow themselves to be interfered with in carrying out their practices, I would state that Sheriff Kitchens himself told my wife and the wife of my son, O. S. Bratton, that even if he should go down onto those plantations and interfere with their laborers that he would be shot down. Attention has also been called to the fact that my life has been threatened and that it had been said publicly that if I dared to enter the county of Phillips that I would be shot down. In support of the statement that my life has been threatened and endangered, I respectfully refer you to Hon. Henry Rector, Assistant United States Attorney, and E. L. McHaney, attorney, both of Little Rock, Arkansas."

The recital of a "system" hardly conveys the human implications in suffering and oppression, cruelties and injustices, which civilized people are prone to think banished from the world until violence and bloody disturbance bring them relentlessly in view. Of the moving stories in Mr. Bratton's report it is possible to recite only one, and that one because it involves not only a victim, but a white jury and a state's attorney:

"I have in mind," says Mr. Bratton, "the case of Ben Donagan, a Negro who lived in Phillips County, where this recent trouble occurred. The question arose between him and one of the managers of the plantation as to his rights in connection with pay for labor done: the manager then told him to leave the place and abandon his crop. The Negro sought the man whom he regarded as the owner of the plantation, laid his case before him, was told by this party to go back and keep out of the way of the manager until a certain time when he would be upon the plantation, at which time it was hoped that the matter could be adjusted. The Negro followed his suggestion. On the appointed day when the party whom the Negro looked upon as owner of the plantation, and who in fact had bargained for it, and immediately after the occurrence became the recognized owner of it, came upon the plantation, the Negro started to meet the manager and the supposed owner. When he was discovered, they both turned, rode directly to him, and upon meeting him the manager deliberately fired into the Negro, shooting him down in the field, having shot him five times. The supposed owner, being a doctor, promptly turned his horse and rode away in the direction in which he and the manager had come. He made no attempt to interfere with the shooting and offered no medical assistance whatever until later he returned and sprinkled some bismuth or some powder of that nature upon the bleeding wounds. The Negro, realizing that he had no hope of relief, unless through the United States courts, applied to us to represent him. We filed suit in the United States court at Helena. . . . The proof was so clear and the instructions to the court such that the jury could not fail to return a verdict, which they did, and assessed the damages for a man being shot five times and made a cripple for life at the sum of one hundred dollars, notwithstanding the fact that the proof was so convincing that the jury could not return a verdict otherwise; still there was no prosecution in the criminal courts, and no indictment against the offenders was filed, although they were undoubtedly guilty of assault with intent to murder *and the then prosecuting attorney of the state courts appeared as one of the defendant's counsel and defended the suit in the United States court.*"

It will be seen that the conditions described in detail by Mr. Bratton coincide with those referred to by "A Southerner" in his letter to *The Memphis Commercial Appeal* and with statements in the Labor Department's report on "Negro Migration in 1916–17." The picture as it is suggested by excerpts from material far too voluminous for embodiment in any but a publication of the federal government places the "Negro insurrection" and "massacre of whites" in different perspective than contemporary press accounts. It shows the entire machinery of civilization in the hands of a white group, many of whose members profit from the exploitation of the black man. It is that group which elects representatives to Congress. It is that group whose voice affects the procedure of the United States, not only with regard to affairs within the country, but in its commerce, industrial and political, with the nations and the peoples of the world. The consideration might give rise to anxious questioning as to the probable fate of the traditions of tolerance, freedom; courage, of the quality of civilization, and the conditions of human life when they are intrusted to such hands.

IX

"SOCIAL EQUALITY" AND SEX

THE Negro in the United States is looked upon by many white persons mainly as a sexual being: he constitutes a menace to the "purity" of the white race; his presence bears a threat of racial amalgamation. Industrial and political relations fade into a sort of unreality when the question of sex is raised as between colored and white people. Among white Americans is developed a species of hysteria: the black man must not invade the white man's sexual preserve. The violent emotions to which sex jealousy gives rise in personal relations find their counterpart in popular outbreaks. For the Negro man there is one unpardonable crime in the United States and that is transgression of the code which makes white women inaccessible to all except white men. In some twenty-nine states[1] marriage between white persons and

[1] According to *The Negro Year-Book for 1918–19*, p. 204.

persons of color is prohibited either by the terms of the state constitution or by statute, and the white man's feelings about "miscegenation" have the sanction of law. The American white man's state of mind has its exact counterpart in many savage or primitive societies. "Inter-tribal marriages were once totally prohibited," says Dennett, writing of native Africans, "but to-day marriages take place, although the offspring of such unions are looked upon much in the same prejudiced light by the Bavili as the offspring of black and white races are looked upon by the Europeans." No free Somali, reports Schurtz,[1] however poor, would marry his daughter to a despised metalsmith, or would himself enter into matrimony with a daughter of that caste. Feeling against race mixture, at its very strongest in North America, has no element that is especially characteristic either of the particular races or of the castes which happen to be involved: the same sort of prohibitions have prevailed and still prevail where no distinctions of color play any part.

Nevertheless, sex relations, the question of the absorption of one race by another, the mingling of colors, are looked upon as the

[1] Heinrich Schurtz, *Das Afrikanische Gewerbe*, Leipzig, 1900, p. 43.

irreducible and final kernel of race problems in the United States. But, as many white Americans would phrase it, the race problem in the United States involves a single simple decision, "Would you allow your daughter to marry a Negro?" If the Negro progresses, acquires a competence and the means to leisure and education, he at the same time assimilates the white man's culture and manners; he threatens to become fit to associate with white men on the basis of any test which white men may erect, except ancestry—and even in the veins of many persons of color flows the blood of the most distinguished white men of the nation's past. The conception of race relations represented by the emphasis upon sex is given extraordinary currency by the press, by politicians who always seek to rouse men's least governable impulses, and by white persons who have absorbed it as part of the credo that clings with all the tenacity of impressions and beliefs absorbed in childhood. In a sense the favorable development of race relations in the United States depends upon the supplanting of this over-simplified issue of sex by other more varied and more immediately pressing considerations.

The process which most gravely menaced establishment of peace and order after the Civil War is still in progress. At that time organizations almost purely political in their intent found a pretext in the "protection of womanhood" from the "Negro fiend." "It is one thing," remarks Professor Hart, "to read of the gallant struggle of the Ku-Klux to protect womanhood and to assert the nobility of the white race; it is quite another to be told, incidentally, that in a certain county of Mississippi the Ku-Klux 'put a hundred and nineteen niggers into the river.' That is what some people call a massacre."

The fury which it was possible to stimulate against Negroes in Omaha, in Washington, in Atlanta, had many contributing elements, industrial and political; but the direct incitement to violence was newspaper report of sexual crime. Persistent endeavors are made to keep this phase of race hatred alive in the South. As late as the spring of 1919 the "Loyal Order of Klansmen," which derived its mummery from the old Ku-Klux, published appeals to white men of the South in the form of huge advertisements in the newspapers. "We are an all-Southern order, for Southern men of white race," said one advertisement, and the order was described as one "that protects the women of our Southland." Beneath the skull and crossbones with its inscription "Ku-Klux Klan" was printed the invitation: "Join the Loyal Order of Klansmen and you solve the problem of law and order in our Southland. With one million men enrolled in the Loyal Order of Klansmen, our land will have peace and security and prosperity. If you wish to make your wives and daughters safe and happy join the Klan to-day. . . ." The quotations are from the Charlotte, North Carolina, *Sunday Observer* of June 22, 1919. This claptrap elicited commendation from the Governor of Mississippi. A Jackson, Mississippi, newspaper, in speaking of the "Loyal Order" as an organization "forming in South Carolina principally for the protection of the white man's womanhood and civilization in the South," quoted Governor Bilbo as follows, "I am strongly impressed with the need of such an organization in the Southland to-day, and wish to be one of the first to join." Southern sentiment was not, however, unanimous with regard to the merits of the resuscitated Ku-Klux Klan. Governor Bickett of North Carolina was quoted in a despatch to *The New York World* of June 30, 1919, as calling upon "all North Carolinians to repudiate this 'desperately wicked appeal to race prejudice.' . . . Governor Bickett's attack," continued the despatch, "which is said to be the first made by any Southern Governor on this organization which is secretly sweeping over the South, comes in the middle of a campaign for membership." Governor Bickett further characterized the undertaking as "a hark back to the lawless time that followed the terrors of the Civil War, and there are paraded before the mind of the readers the terrors of those dark days. The very name that is written on the death head is a subtle appeal to the fears and prejudices of our people. . . . There is no need for any secret order to enforce the law of this land and the appeal to race prejudice is as silly as it is sinful." Wicked, or silly, or sinful, such appeals represent a state of opinion among large numbers of people which is, at the least, responsive. In the South, people's minds are easily wakened to bitter memories, and the ground of hatred does not have to be laid. In the North, a subtler propaganda is necessary. The presumption against the Negro has to be created by singling out sexual crimes of individuals and making them seem characteristic of the race. The process has been adverted to as it was practised in Omaha and in Washington. It accomplished more than local outbreaks, however. It tends to justify terrorism and lynching as practices for "keeping the Negro down" in localities where he is stronger numerically than the white man. Thus, if one were to judge from many editorial statements in Southern newspapers, one would believe that lynching was scarcely ever resorted to except in punishment for the crime of rape against white women. The attitude was well represented in a letter to one of the newspapers of New York in which the writer insisted that "no innocent Negroes are ever mistreated," and in an editorial of the Birmingham, Alabama, *News*, in which it is asserted that "all of these race riots [in the United States] have been caused by the attempts of Negro men to override the race line and to make white women the victims of their lustful passions." In view of the confident assertions which are so frequently made, by Southern editors especially, it is worth while to consider the available evidence on the point. It appears that in the five-year period 1914–18 only 19.8 per cent., or less than one in five Negroes lynched in the United States, was accused of attack or rape committed upon women.[1] Of the 77 Negroes lynched in the United States in 1919, 14, or 18.2 per cent., were accused of assault upon women.[2] It should be borne in mind that in the South "rape" and "intimacy" of a colored man and a white woman are not distinguished in so far as the penalty visited for the offenses. Both are punishable by death for the colored man, frequently by public burning at stake and with ingenious and perverse torture, such as the application to the victim of hot irons, the burning out of his eyeballs with red-hot pokers, and other mutilations which it is needless to describe. During 1919 fourteen colored men were publicly burned by mobs. In one extraordinary, though not unique, case newspapers of several states announced the time of day at which the colored man would be burned, and printed as part of the announcement a statement by the governor of one of the Southern

[1] Lynching statistics from *Thirty Years of Lynching*, published by the National Association for the Advancement of Colored People, New York.

[2] From records of the National Association for the Advancement of Colored People.

states that in the condition of public sentiment he was unable to prevent the murder. The Jackson, Mississippi, *Daily News* of June 26, 1919, announced that the officers of the law had agreed to turn the colored man over to the mob, to be burned alive, without trial: "The officers have agreed to turn him over to the people of the city at four o'clock this afternoon, when it is expected he will be burned." It is the thought of sexual intercourse between colored men and white women that provokes the easily roused fury of many white Americans at the mere mention of "social equality." It is this reservoir of emotion which breaks bounds not only when Negroes commit crimes, but when they are indiscreet enough to prosper. Testimony is overwhelming on the point that the South's color psychosis is rooted in this sex jealousy. It is convenient for political and industrial purposes to have such an easily roused emotionality. Any Negro may be accused of wanting "social equality." Any white man may be accused of being a "nigger-lover" and of desiring "social equality" for Negroes. The Negro who dares to "preach" social equality will be done to death. The white man will be mobbed and driven from the community.

What does the white American mean by social equality? To take the words at their face value, one would suppose he meant association of colored and white persons in the home, personal intercourse without regard to race. In practice the denial of social equality is not confined to personal relations, but includes civil procedure. The socially inferior Negro is exploited on the farm because white lawyers will not take his case against white planters. As soon as the bar of social inferiority is broken down the Negro threatens the white man with competition. A civilization which depends for its economic foundation upon cheap and ignorant labor, which finds it necessary to deny education to large numbers of its colored citizens in order to insure a supply of that cheap and socially inferior labor, cannot face readjustment without grave stresses and strains. Every demand for common justice for the Negro, that he be treated as a human being, if not as a United States citizen, can be and is met with the retort that the demand is for social equality. Instantly every chord of jealousy and hatred vibrates among certain classes of whites—and in the resulting atmosphere of unreasoning fury even the most moderate proposals for the betterment of race relations take on the aspect of impossibilism. By the almost universal admission of white men and of white newspapers, denial of social equality does not mean what the words imply. It means that Negroes cannot obtain justice in many Southern courts; it means that they cannot obtain decent education, accommodation in public places and on common carriers; it means that every means is used to force home their helplessness by insult, which, if it is resisted, will be followed by the administration of the torch or the hempen rope or the bullet.

There is an aspect of social equality which is not often discussed. It involves the position of colored women. White Americans are fond of talking of colored women as unchaste. It is a stigma which is made to attach to all women of color in the United States. Their social inferiority deprives them of the protection which is due their sex, and the "unalterable" opposition of white Americans to social equality is found to be directed only against the colored men. What colored women of the United States have had to endure in silence may yet provide a national drama with the tragedy it has lacked.

Only in very recent years has it begun to dawn upon many white Americans that if the white race is to be kept "pure," white men as well as women must keep it so. A letter to the Birmingham, Alabama, *News* written in October, 1919, states the case bluntly in that the mulatto and "mongrel" race is laid at the door of the white man who "crossed the race line. . . . The sordid details of the race crossing and the inevitable effects on the mind and passion of the inferior race are facts too familiar and repulsive to be enumerated here." The legal barriers to the intermarriage of white and colored people are justified on racial grounds. It is asserted first that the races do not mix, that the resulting mulattoes are "inferior." The position is untenable, as was shown in an earlier chapter. There is no evidence to show that the descendants of race mixture are inferior. On the other hand, those who wish to depreciate the Negro point to the leaders of the Negro as being men of lighter color and ascribe their superiority to the admixture of white blood. The rule will hardly work both ways. As for racial antipathy, its effectiveness is to be questioned in view of the stringent legislation which has been necessary to prevent marriage between white persons and persons of color. In fact, it is a tendency well known to anthropologists and to psychologists, among numbers of developed and heterosexual persons of all races, to seek sexual experience and mates in members of races other than their own. To this tendency white persons of both sexes in the United States are hardly immune. "The North," says Professor Hart, "is often accused of putting into the heads of Southern Negroes misleading and dangerous notions of social equality, but what influence can be so potent in that direction as the well-founded conviction of Negro women that they are desired to be the nearest of companions to white men?" It will be seen that in the present state of information available to white Americans concerning race and race mixture the fury which greets infractions of the sexual code of the South cannot be justified or explained by a deep-rooted "instinct" to keep the white race pure. The barriers to race mixture are primarily social rather than instinctive or racial, and they are fortified by a variety of economic considerations some of which have been indicated.

Why, then, have white men sought out

colored women? In slave days the colored women had little or no protection against the white man. At present, civil and industrial and political disabilities where they are imposed upon Negroes operate to deprive the colored woman of her protection. Frequently colored women do not tell their men of insult offered them by white men because it would be death for the colored man to ask redress. In the spring of 1919 a seventy-two-year-old colored man was hanged by a mob in Georgia because he dared with a gun to defend two terrified colored girls from the advances of two drunken white men who had come late at night into the Negro-residence district. The facts in the case were established by *The Atlanta Constitution.* They represent easily exploitable sexual opportunity for white men of certain communities among colored women. Freudian psychology has an explanation for the strong tendency that has been characteristic of white men of the ruling caste to seek colored women.[1] It rests upon the principle that the choice of the mate is influenced by the characters impressed upon the infant male as belonging to his mother. The mother, being the first woman who

[1] I am indebted for this suggestion to Dr. A. A. Brill of New York.

enters emotionally into the infant's life, provides a first pattern which the man endeavors to find again in his wife. Many Southern men of family were brought up by colored "mammies." So far as their infantile impressions were concerned, a colored face and their mammy's personality represented to them emotionally all that any mother could. Arriving at sexual maturity, the white man, actuated by the mechanism described, found himself impelled toward colored women. At the same time he found a rigid social system discountenancing any legitimate sexual relationship such as marriage. So he had either to repress his impulse by the aid of an exaggerated depreciation of colored people or he indulged and found it necessary to justify himself with the explanation that, being of an inferior race, colored women deserved no better. Thus at once an exception was established to the code of chivalry; and the doctrine of racial inferiority of the Negro was fortified by the emotional mechanism of the individual. To some extent the institution of the mammy is passing and remains chiefly as tarnished glory in the oratorical flights of reminiscent politicians. But that the "mammy complex," owing to the close association of colored women and white infants, had its effect upon the emotional and sex adjustments of white and colored people in the South, there seems strong probability.

To the colored American the problem of sex relations is presented quite differently than to the white. The colored man is the object of the barriers against intermarriage. If white men cannot in many states openly marry Negro women, they may still live with them out of wedlock. But the colored man who should be tempted to illicit sex relations with a white woman bears in mind the violent death that will attend discovery of his indiscretion. He finds that whatever phase of race relations he is involved in, he will probably be accused of claiming "social equality." If the charge can be proved against him, he knows he must die. Much of the increased bitterness that accompanied the induction of American Negroes into the United States army had to do with sex jealousy. Fierce resentment met the status of "equality" with white soldiers that came automatically to colored soldiers. A veritable panic of apprehension and rage swept many white communities at the stories which were widely circulated concerning the intimacy of colored soldiers and white women in France. Fear, which is only another aspect of jealousy, motivated the measures intended to deprive colored troops of social intercourse with white persons in France. Fear brought about the resentful and aggressive determination of the white American to show the Negro that, whatever had occurred in France, he was not to enjoy "social equality" in the United States and that white women were as far as ever beyond the reach of his aspiration. The fact that the fear of intimate relations between colored soldiers and white women was fictitious and bore little relation to the facts did not mitigate the intensity of the feeling. Most colored men, as most colored newspapers, disclaim for the American Negro any general desire to intermarry with members of the white race. The social difficulties imposed upon persons so intermarrying are such that the situation of persons entering upon such a relationship frequently becomes intolerable. If intermarriage between Jew and Gentile offers such social difficulties that they frequently act as deterrents, how much greater the difficulties where there is distinction of color. However, the position in which the colored man is placed in the

United States is a dangerous challenge to his pride. He may have no inclination to any commerce with women not of his own race. But when he is prohibited to have such commerce, when the prohibition is made a symbol of his "inferiority," he cannot fail to resent it. The case was put by Dr. W. E. B. DuBois in *The Crisis* of January, 1920. The Negro might say, according to Doctor DuBois, that he did not *want* to marry a woman of another race "or a woman may say, I do not want to marry this black man, or this red man, or this white man . . . but the impudent and vicious demand that all colored folk shall write themselves down as brutes by a general assertion of their unfitness to marry other decent folk is a nightmare. . . ." The response is what might be expected of any human being to such a prohibition. It may be, and, in present state of race relations undoubtedly is, impracticable that there be intermarriage to any appreciable extent. But in any circumstances the question of intermarriage could more safely be left to the decision of the individuals concerned than to politicians with a vested political interest in race hatred. The difficulties in the way of the Negro's progress are such as to deter most white persons from subjecting themselves to them by marriage. On racial grounds no prohibition of intermarriage has as yet been justified.

What the implications are of the denial of social equality is known to too few Americans. In the Labor Department's report of the migration of Negroes from Georgia in 1916–17 the social causes playing a part are listed as: injustice in the courts, lynching, discrimination in public conveyances, and inequalities in educational advantages. Something of the treatment accorded by white men's courts of the South has been indicated in the story of the Arkansas riots. It is not only when passion runs high, however, that the black man has cause to wonder at and bitterly to resent what the white man euphemistically calls justice. Overzealousness on the part of county and police officials in rounding up Negroes for petty offenses is referred to in the Labor Department's report of the migration from Georgia: "The limit fine or sentence to work the county roads is often imposed." "The abnormal, unwarranted activities of Southern police officers," says another of the Labor Department's investigators, "are responsible for deep grievances among Negroes. In many cases the police have been the tools of powers higher up. Many colored people believe that employers of convicts urge the police to greater activities among Negroes in order to fill up convict camps; and, as if encouraging arrests, the authorities frequently do not pay the constable and other petty officers' salaries for their services, but reward them in accordance with the number of arrests made. Naturally, they get all out of it that the business will stand. The Negro suffers and pays the bill." In the cities the Negro is frequently sentenced on evidence on which a white man would go free. The Negro's testimony rarely, if ever, avails against the white man. But the supreme failure of the white man's system of justice is the ascendancy of the white mob. The emotion which animates the mob has a large component of sex jealousy. Yet lynchings take place on any one of dozens of pretexts. One colored man was lynched in 1919 because he failed soon enough to turn out of the road for white men. The widespread belief in the "racial lust" of the Negro stimulates the fury of a mob. So suggestible is the white man in consequence that many a colored man has been lynched because he followed some white girl or because she imagined it and ran screaming away. The quality of justice which prevails for the colored man in many Southern communities was exemplified in the case of Bragg Williams, who was taken from the Hill County, Texas, jail and publicly burned at stake. He had previously been sentenced to death for murder. "Notice of appeal from the sentence was filed by Williams's attorneys to-day," said the Austin, Texas, *American* of January 20, 1919, "and this action is said to have led the mob to taking the case into its own hands." One mob murder was reported by Walter White, in *The Crisis* of May, 1918, of Jim McIlheron, a prosperous colored man who dared to resent the insults of white men. He defended himself on one occasion, and so doing killed two white men: "Men, women, and children started into the town of Estill Springs from a radius of fifty miles. A spot was chosen for the burning. McIlheron was chained to a hickory-tree while the mob howled about him. A fire was built a few feet away and the torture began. Bars of iron were heated and the mob amused itself by putting them close to the victim, at first without touching him. One bar he grasped, and as it was jerked from his grasp all the inside of his hand came with it. Then the real torturing began, lasting for twenty minutes. During that time, while his flesh was slowly roasting, the Negro never lost his nerve." This occurred in Tennessee in the year 1918. Given such exhibitions and those which accompanied the brutal doing to death of a prosperous colored farmer, Anthony Crawford, at Abbeville, South Carolina, it is not strange that many Negroes came to feel "that character and worth secure no more protection for them than less desirable qualities, and that no Negro is safe." The contempt for the socially "inferior" Negro which makes possible such barbarity as 83 lynchings in 1919 manifests itself in many ways. The exploiter of the Negro can use the denial of social equality for his own purposes, and, as Mr. R. H. Leavell found, "under Southern conditions the employing class can buttress their economic exploitation of the weaker Negro laborer and absolve themselves by appeal to race prejudice, which in many cases seems to have become a sort of religion." As has been pointed out, it is the prosperous Negro against whom the denial of "social equality" is directed. Labor is what is wanted, not human beings. Said Gov. Theodore Bilbo of Mississippi in reply to a query from Chicago: "Your telegram asking how many Negroes Mississippi can absorb received. In reply I desire to state that we have all the room in the world for what we know as 'n-i-g-g-e-r-s,' but none whatever for 'colored ladies and gentlemen.' If these Negroes have been contaminated with Northern social and political dreams of equality, we cannot use them, nor do we want them. The Negro who understands his proper relation to the white man in this country will be gladly received by the people of Mississippi, *as we are very much in need of labor.*"[1] Issuing from the governor of a state, the words might be supposed to represent some small group at least of the population of Mississippi. The indifference to human values which they show, where a dark skin is involved, in fact represents a group far larger than any in Mississippi.

To look upon any man as a source of labor, and inject into relations with his group constant tension which comes of potential fury of sex jealousy, is to involve those relations in the gravest sort of danger. Anything any

[1] *The Crisis,* January, 1920. Quotation from *Chicago Herald-Examiner.*

member of the man's group does may be and often is misinterpreted. The Negro, smarting under the sting of a peculiarly flagrant injustice, if he acts to obtain redress, although his objective may be simply the injustice in question, will be accused by white men of an effort to bring about "social equality"—the objective of the Negro being conceived as white womanhood. By this process the relations of colored and white people of the United States are sexualized to a degree almost unbelievable. It is upon the pretext of the necessity for maintaining the "purity" of the white race that the white supremacy of Southern states is based. It is with this dogma dominant, and the emotions which cling to it, that the South and the nation must face the dilemma of open and deliberate violation of the letter and the spirit of the federal Constitution and its amendments. The editor of the Birmingham, Alabama, *News* pointed out on July 11, 1919, that a reapportionment of representation in accordance not with population, but with votes actually cast, would cost the Southern states 64 Representatives: Alabama, 7; Arkansas, 3; Florida, 2; Georgia, 9; Kentucky, 1; Louisiana, 6; Maryland, 1; Mississippi, 6;

North Carolina, 3; South Carolina, 6; Oklahoma, 2; Tennessee, 3; Texas, 9; Virginia, 6. Whence is derived the resistance to conformity with constitutional amendment and to fortifying the representation of Southern states by having the colored people vote for the men who are supposed to represent them in Washington? Many would answer that the hostility to equal opportunity for Negroes is a consequence of their numerical inferiority in many communities. In fact, as Professor Hart remarked, "the hostility to the Negro is based not on his numbers, but on his supposed inferiority of character," and it is this dogma of inferiority that is used to make more terrible the menace of the Negro's supposed aspirations to social equality and to white womanhood. Upon what is the dogma based? "The Southern whites, with few exceptions, teach no Negroes, attend no Negro church services, penetrate into no Negro society, and they see the Negro near at hand chiefly as unsatisfactory domestic servants, as field hands of doubtful profit, as neglected and terrified patients, as clients in criminal suits or neighborhood squabbles, as prisoners in the dock, as convicted criminals, as wretched objects for the vengeance of a mob." Usually, when a doctrine is so necessary to social order that discussion of the one involves destructive criticism of the other, the doctrine becomes divine. This divinity attaches to the purity of the white race and to white womanhood. The force which Henry Adams conceived to be lacking in American art and letters, the Virgin or Venus, has, by a sort of ironical gesture, condescended to the American political scene. Sex is the motive force which makes the Negro's status dominate the South as a political issue and a question of practical politics. Sex is the distorted glass through which the Negro is presented to view by the press of the country. Southern politics demands a statesmanship of prohibitions and suppressions. The South's color psychosis, which weighs so heavily upon free discussion that the implications of tolerance are known only in small non-political circles, is rooted in the suppression of open discussion of sex and the Negro. Much invective finds its way into public print. But let any one who believes that discussion is possible propose to the Southern Sociological Congress a scientific investigation of the effects of race mixture. In a sense it is true that questions of sex and social equality are at the root of the race problem. They will continue to occasion an easily roused emotionality, at the disposition of cheap politicians and exploiters of labor, just as long as they continue immune to discussion. Just so long as a panic of sexual apprehension seizes communities in which Negroes or white "nigger-lovers" dare to assert that the Negro has any prerogatives which white men, the white man's officers and courts, the white man's society, are bound to respect, just so long will irreconcilable race conflict be rooted in the blind processes of unreason.

Some critic may yet pursue relentlessly the sexlessness and the impotence of American arts and letters. He might recall the picture Samuel Butler drew of a land so dominated by machines that the people finally rose to throw off their oppression, making it a crime to carry so much machinery even as is contained in a watch. In the United States he would find the chief force of sexual expression in jazz. He would find apathetic audiences dragged wondering through musical Parthenons, Gothic cathedrals, Louvres, Pinakotheks, and drawing-rooms, to respond with an appreciative roar to intimations that beyond lay the jungle.

The Negro may be excluded from the dancing-floor, but he plays the music. He may be denied orchestra seats, and still the audience will prefer his composition to Brahms's. He may not vote, he may not mingle socially with white people, but the music to which the jumbled American political scene seems to vibrate and sway is jazz. The South can exclude the Negro from everything but its own thought and emotions and those of the nation.

X

THE NEW NEGRO

THE American Negro, before the World War, was the despair of radicals, even of liberals. In education the mass of colored people had been living on the discarded remnants, both text-books and methods, of white schools. Politically they had all but accepted the belief current in the Southern states that their government was not and would not be a democracy. As individuals, fiercely though their resentment might blaze at brutalities and indignities visited upon men and women of color and at the universal discrimination in industry, they had to acquiesce in the treatment meted out to them. The avenue to power for the colored citizen apparently lay outside politics, in acquiring technical skill, possessions and the influence accompanying them. Negro leadership, especially as it was represented by Booker T. Washington, looked to their becoming indispensable to the nation as toilers—artisans or farmers. The problem of adjusting the race to the American scene was envisaged mainly as one of putting it upon its feet financially. With all except a militant, though growing, minority, emphasis was upon qualifying for the white man's civilization by meeting his economic requirements. Of this adjustment the social implication was a Negro as nearly as possible like the white man, at the expense even of trying to be like the white man. Many a Negro hoped to achieve peace by conformity; therefore conservatism became a sort of norm for colored people in the United States. Social standards are rarely flexible, and the tendency of colored people to adopt those of white persons made for a certain intellectual inflexibility in people otherwise sensitive to suggestion and to the vivid and the new. This and a lasting gratitude toward the Republican party, as representing federal protection for colored people, made what seemed to be a solid block of conservatives of colored people in the United States. Economically, the attitude had value and bore fruit. Even its bitterest critics admit the accomplishments of trade and agricultural schools. Many colored people were enabled to leave behind them the wasting hazards of casual and exploited labor. Many, having obtained business training, taught their fellows or advanced their own fortunes. The story of Tuskegee, as Booker Washington has told it, has much that should give to every generous American pride and inspiration.

But Negroes in the United States found the attempt at economic progress alone insufficient. That progress was checked by the barriers of the white man's civilization. As early as 1910 and before then, groups of colored people and their white friends realized that the white man's political power could be used to nullify the Negro's economic progress. With a dominant and aggressive white minority in control, after 1876, not only of the ballot and political machinery, but of courts, no colored man's progress became secure. Given agrarian conditions such as are illumined by the Arkansas disorders, with the impossibility of obtaining redress and the absence of adequate education, and it was obvious numbers of colored people had little or no opportunity for advancement. Add to political and civil disabilities social discrimination directed especially against the successful individual of color, and Booker Washington's avenue to freedom became perilously insecure. One of the most forceful of Washington's critics, Dr. W. E. B. DuBois, soon came to the conclusion that if the Negro was to find existence in the United States tolerable he must boldly demand and conquer for himself full civil rights and the ballot. In the development of political consciousness of the Negro in the United States Doctor DuBois and his periodical, *The Crisis*, played an important part. Pride and assertion of the dignity of manhood and womanhood for individuals of the race came from him and found increasing response among colored people throughout the nation. Doctor DuBois took American professions at their face value, and inquired pointedly and bitterly into mob violence and lynching, into segregation, disfranchisement, and discrimination. Accompanying the spiritual revolt from what many colored people regarded as the submissiveness of Booker Washington and his followers—a willingness to acknowledge the superiority of the white man—came the rapid growth of a Negro middle class, with its professional men, its industrial leaders, and its urban standards of life and social intercourse. A Negro press grew until there were few communities so small as to be untouched by some publication edited by and for colored people. It is invidious to measure the progress of any group of people by its economic standing: philosophy, fable, and the most moving of the world's poetry and songs have come from slaves. But the Negro's economic status conditioned his political consciousness in the United States. Thus, it is significant that in the decade 1900 to 1910, whereas the number of Negroes in agricultural pursuits increased 35 per cent., the increase in trade and transportation amounted to 103 per cent., and in manufacturing and mechanical pursuits to 156 per cent. The increase of 186 per cent. represented a rise in the number of Negroes engaged in industry from 275,149 to 704,174. Mr. Monroe Work has published a statistical abstract of fifty-three years of progress of the Negro in the United States. His figures show an increase in the number of homes owned from 12,000 in 1866 to 600,000 in 1919. In the same period colored people increased the number of farms they operate by 980,000. In *The Negro Year-Book for 1918–19* Mr. Work estimated the number of Negroes engaged in business enterprises as not less than 50,000, exclusive of more than 10,000 boarding- and lodging-house keepers. An illuminating parallel of the industrial advance of the Negro in fifty years shows him engaged in 37 sorts of business in 1867 and in 187 kinds of business in 1917. In the latter year his enterprises included automobile service and garage, contracting and building, hotelkeeping, lumber business, real estate, and banking, tailoring, stock-raising, and theaters. Insurance, according to Mr. Work, one of the most important forms of business activity of American Negroes, is conducted by their own companies, of which one had $1,944,910 insurance in force in 1915. For the bourgeoisie thus developing, a press was essential. Mr. Work listed some 450 periodicals published by or for Negroes in the United States, of which 220 were newspapers and 7 were magazines of general literature. Among the foremost of the Negro newspapers in the United States are *The Chicago Defender* with a nation-wide circulation of more than 150,000, *The New York Age* and *The News*, *The Colorado Statesman*, the Atlanta (Georgia) *Independent*, *The St. Louis Argus*, *The Pittsburgh Courier*, and *The Richmond Planet*. The development of the Negro press in the United States represents in part business enterprise. But its astonishing success, the multiplicity of tiny and obscure sheets in small communities, as well as the avid reception of powerful organs like *The Chicago Defender* in the South, represent a well-founded distrust of the accounts of Negro doings in the white press. As late as December, 1919, the Associated Negro Press sent a news story to its subscribers, pointing out that in an Associated Press (white) report of a new diving apparatus which would enable salvage operations at hitherto unattempted depths, the fact had been omitted that the inventor was a Negro. Frequently accounts of racial troubles which appear in the Negro press contradict the assertions or the implications to be drawn from statements in the white press. Where a propaganda occurs in the white press such as helped bring about the disorders in Omaha, Washington, and Chicago, the Negro press vigilantly runs down exaggerations and misstatements. Frequently, as has been said, the Negro is better informed of the cause and the nature of race conflict than is the white man. Exaggerations occur on both sides. The Negro press, with a few exceptions, has not the machinery or the means which make possible the largest white news services, and bitterness more often shows itself obviously in the presentation of news in the Negro press than in the white. The distinction, however, is one of subtlety rather than of standards. White newspapers have nothing to teach the Negro press of fairness in the treatment of news of race relations.

How important the Negro press has been in the process of the Negro's becoming politically articulate can be measured by the statements of white men. Magazines like *The Crisis* and *Challenge*, newspapers like *The Defender*, are cordially execrated among white men in the South. An article in *The Defender* was held responsible for the riot in Longview, Texas. Gov. Charles Brough of Arkansas said he believed *The Crisis* and *Defender* were responsible for the Arkansas riots and announced his intention of asking the Postmaster-General to exclude them from the mails. Measured by the editorial utterances of their haters and detractors, Negro editors have been potent indeed, for they are credited with the power of creating the most violent conflicts that American communities have known, short of war. It will be seen that before the war the American Negro had the nucleus at least of a fully evolved bourgeois society. Representatives of his race served the government as legal officers, as consular agents with diplomatic responsibilities. Poets of the race, Paul Laurence Dunbar, James Weldon Johnson; entertainers and actors among whom Bert Williams stands out; essayists and critics of the caliber of William Stanley Braithwaite and Doctor DuBois; musicians of the rank of R. Nathaniel Dett, J. Rosamond Johnson, Harry Burlcigh—havc a place in American civilization independent of any condescension to their Negro blood. Whether or not the American musical comedy is an art form or merely a form of dissipation is a question subject to the vagary of individual taste. That it has been the medium through which countless Americans have experienced what passes for instrumental music, the dance, song, gaiety is indubitable. To no small degree is the development of American musical comedy, its intriguing rhythms and its popular songs, due to colored composers and librettists. In the gap between American idealism and the hard-boiled soul of American practicality the American Negro has interposed his warmth and vivacity. More and more the Negro spirituals and plantation melodies, debased and all but obscured by jazz, are coming seriously into their own on the concert stage and in the works of serious composers. It is not here a question of comparative merit. The Negro has introduced human values into American civilization of a sort in which it has been found peculiarly lacking. The Negro plays, sings, dances for the love of what he is doing and experiencing. In this he is fitted to become the teacher and a vivifying force in a civilization preoccupied by ulterior motives.

It will be seen that in all but name the "new Negro" was already in existence, a far cry from the humble servitor, the "good old darky," the mythical personality compounded of servility, vice, and gratitude. If between the evolved and educated Negro citizen and the drifting roustabout of the far South yawns the interval between the primitive and the civilized, that same gap is observable among white men in New York City. It is almost needless to remind that the manner of the Aurignacian age sometimes disguises itself in the language of United States Senators. The "new Negro," then, is a name not so much for a being brought into existence during the World War as for that being's awareness of himself and his immediate problems. Certain colored men, notably A. Philip Randolph and Chandler Owen, editors of *The Messenger*, a monthly magazine, gave the term special significance in that they applied it to the class-conscious, revolutionary Socialist whom they in part represented, but mainly hoped to evoke. They took their theory and their terminology from orthodox Marxian Socialism and preached that in the class war, in the identification of the Negro worker with working-class solidarity and revolution, lay the only solution of the Negro question in the United States. This left wing represented the farthest swing away from the accommodating optimism of Booker Washington. It repudiated even Doctor DuBois and *The Crisis*, together with all reform movements for the advancement of the Negro under the capitalist system. *The Messenger* urged the Negro's identity of interest with the Industrial Workers of the World, as a worker for the most part unskilled, without political rights, disfranchised, and exploited. "The chief need of the Negro is the organization of his industrial power," said *The Messenger* of October, 1919. Emphasis was again laid upon the importance to the Negro of his economic might. But new standards of criticism had come into the Negro press with *The Messenger*. Urging class solidarity, the editors at the same time mercilessly criticized their own race, its church, its leadership. The men who had led the struggle against lynching, civil disabilities, and disfranchisement were held up for observation to the "new Negro" as accepters of the capitalist state. And against that state the onus of *The Messenger's* criticism was directed. Doctor DuBois, Prof. Kelly Miller, Archibald H. Grimke, William Pickens, James Weldon Johnson, and other leaders of Negroes in the United States met what might be called severe praise at the hands of the editors of *The Messenger*. Radicalism, for *The Messenger*, was the measuring-stick for future leadership toward the full emancipation of the Negro. As the old leaders showed themselves susceptible to the economic interpretation of social forces they were justified; otherwise their failings were ruthlessly commented upon. In a scathing reply to Representative Byrnes of South Carolina, who raised the cry of "radicalism" among Negroes which the white press and the Department of Justice took up, the editors of *The Messenger* stated their position in unequivocal terms: "Washington is no more, and with him has passed the old me-too-boss, hat-in-hand, good nigger which you and your ilk so dearly love. The radical Negro leaders have the ear and the hand of the masses. The New Crowd Negroes think no more of Moton [Maj. Robert Moton, head of Tuskegee] than they do of you and Cole Blease and Vardaman! They look upon him as a 'good-nigger' puppet. We are also appealing to the manly passions of the Negroes and inspiring them to act on the manly and lawful principle of self-defense in the protection of their homes, their lives, and their property." As to the charge of Bolshevism which Representative Byrnes made, the editors had this to say: "We would be glad to see a Bolshevik government substituted in the South in place of your Bourbon, reactionary, vote-stolen, misrepresentative Democratic régime. . . . Negroes perform most of the service in the South. . . . Under the Soviet system, their right to vote would be based upon their service and not upon race or color." In *The Messenger* unequivocal demands for full equality of every sort, civic, political, social, found voice.

There is an advantage in being doctrinaire

familiar to the propagandist social revolutionary. Something more than doctrinaire pungency, however, appeared in *The Messenger*. Its editors envisaged the American Negro not merely as a member of a closed group, isolated and hemmed in, suffering from and protesting at injustice, but as a full citizen of the world with a part in its economic and political conflicts. With the instrument of economic determinism at their hand, the editors of *The Messenger* embarked upon a raking criticism of attitudes and achievements among members of their own race. In a sense they carried on Doctor DuBois's insurgence from the Booker Washington leadership. Like Doctor DuBois, they set out to create new habits of thought among American Negroes, and, like him, they represented an attitude which had grown ripe for expression. Their attitude is shared by many colored workers disillusioned with the disingenuousness of conservative labor as represented in some unions of the American Federation of Labor. It is shared by many cultured and educated Negroes who find themselves, by the terms of race discrimination, fighting shoulder to shoulder with the humblest people of color.

It will be noted that the growth of radical sentiment, the determination that race relations must be fundamentally altered in the United States, was not sudden. Every Negro leader of any vitality was forced to be a radical from the point of view of the reactionary groups of white people prepared to concede nothing. But the most potent force in precipitating radicalism was the entrance of the United States into the World War. The treatment of the colored soldier by Americans in France and in their own country has been referred to, as has been the exploitation of colored people under the powers conferred by "work or fight" laws. Not many Negroes became as articulate in their disillusion as the editors of *The Messenger*. But disillusion set in that was nation-wide. The firm hold which the Republican party had held on the gratitude of the mass of colored people began to be loosened. The consequence was not the creation of any definite new political alignments, but rather of an unstable equilibrium in which colored people took stock of their resources and powers and became increasingly aware of themselves as a potential voting block. In all the disorders that took place in 1919 the Negro fought in self-protection. He no longer relied on promises or on protection even of the federal government. With a Democratic administration in power, the Negro had little to hope from federal protection during and immediately after the World War. In the National Capital Jim-Crowism had crept in. Negroes were not served in the restaurants of the capital, and they found the attitude of the South reflected everywhere in Washington. They found the Department of Justice being used, not to examine into deplorable conditions which had brought about race riots, but to trace the tenuous connections between "Reds," I. W. W., and the Negro, and to proclaim Negro insurrection and radicalism to a willing press and a credulous public. It is emancipation to distrust others and to rely upon oneself. Never, perhaps, in the history of the country was there more distrust of American white men by Negroes than after the World War. They had taken the measure of the white press and its news-distributing organizations. They had seen local government crumble and brutality rein almost unchecked except by their own bullets. They had seen the federal government, through its one department articulate on their affairs, pursue not their oppressors, but those who were voicing their heartfelt, burning sense of injustice. Something of the ethics of real politics was borne in upon the American Negro by the treatment accorded him. Nowhere, perhaps, was the American Negro's position brought to more dramatic focus than before two United States Senators in Washington in January, 1920. The Senators were conducting a hearing on a resolution introduced by one of them, providing for a Congressional investigation into mob violence and lynching in the United States. The evidence had been given. Statistics and stories of horror lay in the typewritten sheets on the table. And the question raised was one of jurisdiction. A Senator pointed out that the interpretation placed by the courts upon the Constitution and constitutional amendments prevented legislation by states infringing personal liberty, but gave the federal government no power to act in protection of that liberty. The Senators paused. A white-haired gentleman rose. His face was dark in color as if he had been deeply sunburnt. "Gentlemen," he said, in effect, "we come to you deeply aggrieved by injustice. The states have failed to protect us. The federal government professes itself powerless. I am an old man of seventy years. I have served my country abroad. I have passed through almost every phase of government service, and, like many another of my race, have given freely of myself. Yet when we come to you, in behalf of twelve million American Negroes, you tell us there is no redress for our wrongs. What are we to expect? What are we to hope for?" A Senator hastened to express interest, sympathy, his desire to remedy the conditions set down in the documents before him. But the questions: "What are we to expect? What are we to hope for?" remained unanswered.

No intelligent answer to the question put by that colored leader has yet been attempted. In a sense there is no solution of the problems of race relations, even on paper and by Northern dilettanti. It is idle to say, give the Negro his full rights, when the granting of those rights lies with an illiterate white electorate at the mercy of brutal and vituperative editors. Yet approaches to the problems have been made. It is coming to be realized that the problems of race relations can be and must be cleft vertically into the constituent problems of democracy: a free press serving the people with news, not rumor and innuendo; real representation and control by the electorate over their elected representatives; proprietorship by the producer not only in political fictions, but in the industrial processes which depend upon him and by which he lives. To this extent the "new Negro," as he is represented in *The Messenger*, has affirmed a significant and vital fact: there is no race question independent of other problems of democracy; race relations constitute democracy's most essential problem, a problem compounded of all the other adjustments which free men are called upon to make in forming and maintaining social relations. Shameful as was the year 1919, with bloodshed, lynching, and race riot in the United States, its function was still to bring before the attention of the nation that a national problem, long unsolved, demanded serious attention. A condition which had been glossed over, the illegal disfranchisement by methods of terrorism of millions of colored Americans, was brought boldly to light. The Negro became aware of his economic power. The white South came to know that in losing Negro labor it was allowing to slip away the very foundation of its productivity and prosperity. And in a few communities the lesson had already been learned by white Americans that their colored neighbors were able and were eager to co-operate in establishing decent conditions under which white men and men of color could live in peace and security.

Halting steps were taken in 1919 and early in 1920 to attack the most obvious of race maladjustments. Two resolutions, one in the Senate and one in the House of Representatives, providing for Congressional investigation of lynching and race riots, and a number of bills which would make lynching a crime under federal jurisdiction, showed the increasing attention directed toward race relations. The steps proposed were laudable, but would leave the mainsprings of racial maladjustment untouched. The experience of Atlanta and of Chicago after their race riots might well be drawn upon by the nation. Here, joint bodies of colored and white men met to devise means for making mob violence in the streets of their city impossible. In Illinois, after the Chicago riots, and in Arkansas the governors of the states appointed commissions to investigate into the causes of the disturbances. Communities in the South have discovered the advantage in forming joint bodies of white and colored citizens to deal with matters of local concern. In the course of such conferences as have been held, both white and colored men have made interesting discoveries about one another. White men have been impressed with the administrative ability of their colored neighbors. Colored men have found, often to their astonishment, a body of white men eager to give them fair treatment and equal opportunity.

Unfortunately, the growth of local co-operation must remain slow. It depends largely upon the emancipation of the American people from their newspapers. Little is to be expected from the federal government. At the hearing in Washington called to inquire into the need for investigating lynching and race riots, one Senator took occasion to read into the record an effusion from the Department of Justice ascribing race riots to the activities of "Reds." Not even the Department of Justice, however, had the temerity to connect "Reds" with lynching. So long as the complexion of the national legislature is determined on the basis of open and flagrant disregard of amendments to the federal Constitution and violation of their provisions, little is to be hoped or expected from that source. The Republican party in its endeavor to invade the solid Democratic South finds it necessary to pander to the South's color psychosis through its "lily-white" state organizations. In the old political parties there is hope neither for the Negro nor for the white man who desires a decent approach to the problems of race relations.

The future of race relations, in so far as they are not allowed to degenerate into violence and irremediable bitterness, would seem to lie with labor and with liberal political forces that represent working-class sentiment as the old parties do not and cannot. It will be largely on the job and in the labor union that the identity of interest of the colored worker and the white will be demonstrated, probably despite all efforts to maintain the color line in industry by using unorganized colored men to break white strikes. A tolerable future for the relations between white and colored people in the United States depends for the most part upon white labor. The Negro has found a place in industry. He has discovered his strategic importance in the contest of capital and labor. He has armed himself for self-defense and is prepared to fight. Pushing the issue to sporadic and embittered clashes between white and colored people in the United States involves a sort of smoldering civil war that no American can contemplate with anything but deep concern and anxiety. If white unions have learned from the northward migration of Negroes, they will ignore the propaganda in the white press; they will attempt to break down the Negro's distrust of the American labor union by giving him the square deal.

In so far as the South is concerned, conditions improve as the Negro moves out. The migration northward continued after the war and was still in full progress early in 1920. Yet such testimony as that published by Mr. T. Arnold Hill, referred to in an earlier chapter, indicates little, if any, improvement in the treatment of colored people as a direct consequence of their services in the war. The statement of the Governor of Mississippi that "niggers," not colored men and women, were wanted in his state indicates little perception of the change of mind and attitude that is imperative. One is forced to the conclusion that in many parts of the South he Negro can expect decency only when his bsence has hurt the prosperity of his white eighbors. When white planters offer to uild schools as an inducement to Negroes o stay on the farms and to return from ities of the North, as they announced late n 1919, it is a sign that the beginning of a esson has been learned. The sort of minority pinion from which much that is hopeful of etter race relations emanates is represented y a group of professors in Southern universities, known as the University Commission n Race Questions. Among the institutions epresented on the commission were the Universities of Alabama, Arkansas, Florida, Georgia, Louisiana, Mississippi, South Caroina, and Texas. The commission published four open letters to college men of the South in which lynching, education, the migration, and reconstruction were treated forcibly and with courage. These Southern professors pointed out that of fifty-two persons lynched in 1914, "only seven—two white and five colored—or 13 per cent., were charged with the crime against womanhood." Lynching they termed a "contagious social disease, and as such is of deep concern to every American citizen and to every lover of civilization." They pointed out ruthlessly that "in at least four cases," of lynching in 1915, "it later was discovered that the victims of the mob were innocent of the crime of which they were accused." In the letter on education, dated September 1, 1916, the commission pointed out that "inadequate provision for the education of the Negro is more than an injustice to him; it is an injury to the white man" in that it made for inefficiency. The letter on the migration, written in 1917, made clear that humane treatment would be effective in stopping the exodus. In the final communication, entitled "A New Reconstruction," dated April 26, 1919, the commission urged "a more general appreciation of the Negro's value as a member of the community," alluded to his services in the World War, and spoke of "a splendid record of which the Negroes and their white friends may be justly proud." Despite a faint suggestion of patronizing tone, the communications of these professors represent a spirit that, if it is given expression, will make it possible for white and black to live amicably side by side. But such a point of view is too often submerged in the clamor of the press.

Little has been said thus far of the need in the United States of systematic information on matters concerning colored people and their relation to white people. Investigations conducted by men of science have been few. The political obstacle to the truth about race and race relations weighs upon the universities of the North, even. An anthropologist of international repute told me late in 1919 that he bad for years been endeavoring to stimulate interest in university studies to be undertaken among American Negroes, with a view to making important racial determinations of various sorts. He had about given over his efforts because the universities feared to antagonize those of their benefactors who had preconceived notions on the subject of race and race relations. Yet the crying need for even elementary facts is evident. White people who call themselves educated are subject to the most amazing delusions and prejudices with regard to race, and especially with regard to their own colored neighbors. If there were not this almost universal ignorance, colored by the back-stairs gossip of newspapers, there would hardly be occasion for such a volume as this. The misconceptions which are at the root of race prejudice and violence would long since have evaporated. But violence and prejudice perpetuate themselves by preventing the acquisition of any reliable body of fact. It is only from a realization on the part of Americans white and colored that the poison of color hatred affects every phase of American life, vitiates politics, is used to intrench exploiting classes, to further the plans of self-seeking politicians and editors, to foster the intolerance and parochialism which make for imperialism and wars of aggression, that any demand for right can spring. On the face of race relations now is written the word "menace." With any but the sort of appointees that are to be expected from the Republican or Democratic parties, one would be tempted to urge as an immediate step the creation of a federal department of race relations, with a Cabinet officer responsible not only for investigating maladjustments where they show themselves, but for initiating campaigns of the information and education of which the body of United States citizens are sorely in need. The one experiment in that direction undertaken by the federal government, the Bureau of Negro Economics of the Department of Labor, was permitted virtually to go out of existence for lack of appropriations of funds to carry on its valuable and useful work.

The chief problem of race relations in the United States is the education of white people to decency in their attitude toward colored citizens. The nation will never be made whole in its own conscience while overt lawlessness stalks in the United States Senate and the House of Representatives. Hypocrisy must be of the very essence of American public life while the word democracy and disfranchisement of Negroes, ideals of liberty and oppression of colored people under the guise of denying them "social equality," are juxtaposed; while white men take their freedom with colored women and torture with bestial cruelty any colored man who has committed the crime of attracting a white woman's regard. The first step in an approach to the problems of race relations will be a demand upon the part of United States citizens for information, exact information not only of the anthropologist, but with regard to the treatment of colored men and women by white men and women in the United States. When those facts are made known, as some effort has been made to suggest them in this survey, American public opinion will demand a change amounting to revolution. If such a demand is not made, antagonism between white and colored people, played upon for political and chiefly for economic and industrial purposes, bolstering inefficiency, ignorance, and Prussianism in the South, infecting the entire people with intolerance, will become one of many forces disintegrating any orderly progress of civilization. Truly the United States stands with problems of race before its people which, as Mr. Harold Stearns has observed, the Civil War did not solve, but created. It rests with informed and intelligent minorities, with class-conscious laborites, colored and white, to rescue the relations between white and colored Americans from the embitterment into which they threaten to gravitate. Meanwhile the American Negro, disillusioned, newly emancipated from reliance upon any white savior, stands ready to make his unique contribution to what may some time become American civilization.

APPENDIX

REPORT ON SITUATION AT BOGALUSA, LOUISIANA, BY PRESIDENT OF LOUISIANA STATE FEDERATION OF LABOR

(Transmitted to the National Association for the Advancement of Colored People by Frank Morrison, Secretary American Federation of Labor, in letter dated February 4, 1920.)

THE Great Southern Lumber Company who [*sic*] own the lumber mills and the pulp and paper mills at Bogalusa, Louisiana, are perhaps the largest lumber producers in the United States. They claim that the sawmill located at Bogalusa is the largest mill in the world. They are also connected with several large enterprises; they are interested in the large mill located at Virginia, Minnesota, which they claim to be the next largest mill in the world.

About three years ago they put in a very large pulp and paper mill at the Bogalusa plant, and about that time the workmen at Bogalusa began to try to organize. They asked for organizers, and several attempts were made to help the people there. About this time a young man named Rodgers, an organizer for the carpenters and joiners, went to Bogalusa and while there was arrested as a suspicious character. He was released after getting the news to some of his friends in New Orleans; however, they claimed that he was a dangerous character and filed charges against him in the federal court and while he was in jail at

Bogalusa, the Bogalusa officers had put dynamite caps and fuse in his grip. This grip was produced in the federal court as evidence, but their case was so flimsy and so crude that the federal authorities dismissed it without trial. Later James Leonard, at that time vice-president of the State Federation of Labor and an organizer of the A. F. of L., went to Bogalusa and was told by the authorities there that they would not permit any organizer to come there and organize the men. Mr. Leonard left Bogalusa and returned to New Orleans; however, this did not stop the desire of the workers at Bogalusa, who were in touch with the state federation; and later on W. M. Donnells was sent there as an organizer for the carpenters, and organized the carpenters of the place. Then, in rapid succession, the organization of all lines followed until we had seventeen local unions at the place with a splendid central union.

Seeing that the men had organized in spite of their efforts to thwart it, the company became furious and tried to intimidate the members of the locals; finding that this would not work they then started systematic system of discharging all white union men and putting non-union Negroes to work in their places and at the same time making a great deal of noise and trying to work up a spirit of antagonism to the organization of Negroes, even telling the farmers and planters that we were trying to organize the Negro farm laborers. This forced the hand of labor and a campaign of organization was then begun to organize the Negroes in the employ of the Great Southern Lumber Company. This brought on quite a little feeling. The company called a mass-meeting of the citizens, where several public men, among them a Congressman, made speeches opposing the organization of Negroes. Donnells spoke at that meeting and defended the right of labor to organize. Seeing that the men were determined the company then entered into an agreement to the effect that they would stop discharging the union men if they would cease organizing Negroes. This arrangement was made with the understanding that no union man should be discriminated against or prejudiced in any way because of his membership in a union. This arrangement had not been made thirty days when the company immediately started discharging both white and colored union men, and issued an ultimatum from Mr. W. S. Sullivan, the vice-president and general manager of the plant, that he would not recognize any union man and that he would not meet nor confer with any one representing union labor and instructed his office to so inform Donnells and others.

This agreement was made in April of 1919, and from that time on things happened fast at Bogalusa. Mr. Sullivan, who is vice-president of the Great Southern Lumber Company, is also mayor of the town of Bogalusa. He then placed about thirteen of his henchmen that had not joined labor on the police force of the town. They were augmented by a number of deputies appointed by the sheriff of the parish, and then began a reign of terror in the town.

They tried to get rid of all the leaders by terrorizing them and by offering them bribes to leave the place. Finding this would not work, they sent their employment man to Chicago and other cities to secure three thousand Negroes, with the intent of placing non-union Negroes in the industries there and forcing the union men to leave. They failed to get any men in Chicago; I was informed by reliable parties in Chicago that they did not offer sufficient wages and that the men were informed that no labor trouble existed. However, the men knew that they were wanted as strike-breakers and would not go. On failing to get men, they immediately began arresting men, both black and white, on all kinds of trumped-up charges and taking them to the county seat about twelve miles away. The automobiles furnished the police and deputy sheriffs were used for the purpose of taking the men to the county seat, but the men when discharged for lack of evidence had to get back to Bogalusa any way they could. In addition to this, several men were beaten by these same gunmen; others were ordered to leave, while some of them were offered bribes to leave.

Previous to this, a committee had been appointed, two by the company and two by the men, to investigate wages and working conditions in the lumber industry throughout the state and east Texas and western Alabama and Mississippi. This committee reported that the Great Southern Lumber Company was paying less wages than any mill west of the Mississippi River. One of the men representing the company was a sawyer, who had at that time never joined the union. However, when he was selected by the company to represent, he accepted and when the report was made he was accused by the company of not making a fair report. He then joined the Sawyers' Union and was soon made president of the union. They then tried to induce him to leave. He owned his own home in the town and also a small farm just outside of the city. He was told by the henchmen of the company that he had better sell his property and leave the place. He refused to do this, and while attending a meeting he was called from the hall, when seven of the gunmen attacked him, placed him in an automobile, and ran him five miles out of town, where they took him out of the car and there proceeded to beat him into an almost unconscious condition. They then dictated a letter which they compelled him to write to his wife, telling her to sell all their property and leave at once, as he was not coming back. This man, whose name is Ed. O'Bryan, was then taken to a station on the Northeastern Railroad and placed on the car bound for New Orleans, and was told by the gunmen that they were the Department of Justice agents, and that he was under arrest by the federal authorities as an I. W. W. agitator. They had, in the mean time, painted a sign on the man's back which read "I am an I. W. W.," and when placed on the train they found Brother Donnells on the same train. They also told him that both he and O'Bryan were under arrest by the federal authorities as I. W. W. agitators. They held guns on both of them, and would not allow them to speak to each other. At the first station out of New Orleans, two of the gunmen got off the car while one stayed on. On reaching the yards in the city, this man also got off and left O'Bryan and Donnells alone.

After having O'Bryan's wounds treated, they went to the office of the Superintendent of the Department of Justice and filed complaints from which nothing has yet been heard.

The president of the Colored Timber Workers' Union was another one they offered a small sum of money to leave and sell his property. He owned a home and some live stock in the place, all told valued at about thirty-five hundred. They offered him two thousand to sell this property and leave. He refused to do so. They went that night to his house and shot it to pieces, and searched for him. However, he had told the white labor people of the offer to leave and they had gotten him away. When they could not find him, they then blamed the white labor people for getting him away and then gave out a statement to the press that Lum Williams and another labor sympathizer had paraded the Negro Dacus up and down the street while they were heavily armed, and had defied the authorities to arrest him. I am informed by a number of people, who are not members of labor, that this is a false statement, as nothing of the kind was done, and the gunmen who claimed to have a warrant for the arrest of Dacus had nothing but a trumped-up charge. That was their excuse for going to Lum Williams's place on the following day where they murdered Williams, who was president of the Central Trades Council, together with three others. The claim of the gunmen that the union men had arms in the building was untrue, as there was not a gun in the building. They drove up in their automobiles and without warning began to shoot. Williams was the first to appear at the door where he was shot dead, without a word being spoken by either side. Two other men, who were in his office at the time, were shot down, and the bodies of the three men fell one on top of the other in the doorway. The other men attempted to leave the building by the back door where two of them were shot down while coming out with their hands above their heads; the only shot fired by any man connected with the labor people in any way was fired by a young brother of Lum Williams who shot Captain LeBlanc in the shoulder with a .22-caliber rifle, after he had shot his brother to death. This Captain LeBlanc was a returned soldier and was placed in command of the gunmen in Bogalusa. One of the men wounded at the back door of the building where the killing occurred was taken to the sanitarium where he died three days later, but no one was allowed to see him while he was alive.

Young Williams was arrested immediately and charged with shooting with intent to kill, while the thirteen gunmen, who did the murder, were not arrested until three weeks later, when the grand jury took action and bound them over to await the final action of the regular session of the grand jury in May. They were immediately released on a bond of forty thousand dollars each and have returned to Bogalusa where they are still armed and defying the law of the state.

They have been continually arresting Negroes for vagrancy and placing them in the city jail. It seems that a raid is made each night in the section of the town where the Negroes live and all that can be found are rounded up and placed in jail charged with vagrancy. In the morning the employment manager of the Great Southern Lumber Company goes to the jail and takes them before the city court where they are fined as vagrants and turned over to the lumber company under the guard of the gunmen where they are made to work out this fine. There is now an old Negro in the hospital at New Orleans whom they went to see one night, and ordered to be at the mill at work next day. The old man was not able to work, and was also sick at the time. They went back the next night and beat the old man almost to death and broke both of his arms between the wrist and elbow. This old man was taken from the hospital and went to the county seat and appeared before the grand jury and the papers made a big thing of it and said we were trying to stir up race trouble. The State Federation has taken the matter up with labor throughout the state and we intend to fight the thing to a finish.

However, we are badly handicapped for funds to fight the combined forces of the entire lumber industry, as they have organized an organization to fight us and now have a man named Boyd, who was editor of *The Lumbermen's Journal*, traveling through the

Southern lumber states forming local organizations with the sole purpose of defending the Great Southern Lumber Company and fighting any attempt on the part of labor to organize the lumber industry in the South. I have it from reliable sources that they have succeeded in lining up the hardwood-lumber people also in this anti-union organization. They are holding meetings in all the towns in the Southern lumber states.

We have employed the Hon. Amos L. Ponder as an attorney to defend young Williams for the shooting and to prosecute the thirteen gunmen. We are having some investigating done and hope to be able to bring them to justice along with those who are responsible for the many outrages against humanity and justice. However, they are still terrorizing the people that live in Bogalusa, and just last week Brother Donnelly was on his way, in company with Brother Donnells, to Bogalusa to hold a meeting. Brother Donnelly is now president of the central body at that place. On arriving at the depot in New Orleans one of the gunmen met them there and told Donnells that if he went to Bogalusa he would be murdered, and made several threats. They had him arrested on two charges—one for threatening to kill and one for carrying concealed weapons. He was released on bond in each case and, no doubt, no effort will ever be made to have him appear for trial in New Orleans.

The union men asked the Governor of the state to have federal troops sent to Bogalusa, which he did, and which no doubt prevented bloodshed, as it seemed that the Southern Lumber Company had determined to get rid of all members of labor . . . Some of the citizens had become aroused over the matter, on one side or the other, till it looked as though a serious situation had been reached, and should the troops be taken away and the gunmen begin again their reign of terror, it is almost certain that the citizens will take a hand in the affair. Some of them are friendly to labor while some of them are aiding the gunmen in every way they can. The citizens of the parish have requested that marshall law [martial law] be declared, but at present under that authority of the constitution governing such matters, the Governor cannot declare the parish under marshall law [martial law] as the authorities there are now keeping order. It seems this is being done to assist the lumber company in its effort to have the soldiers removed, as Sullivan is trying to get the soldiers away from there until such time as we are assured that the local civil authorities will see that the laws are enforced and justice can be had.

This report does not cover all details of the case, but will give you some idea of the conditions that prevail in Bogalusa, and in the entire Southern lumber belt. This will happen anywhere in the Southern belt if they get away with it at Bogalusa, for they are the one industry in this country that have always resisted organization to the finish.

[Signed] T. J. GREER,
President Louisiana State Federation of Labor

THE END

www.ingramcontent.com/pod-product-compliance
Lightning Source LLC
Chambersburg PA
CBHW040144270326
41929CB00024B/3366